As the Ink *Flows*

DEVOTIONS
to Inspire
Christian Writers
& Speakers

Glenda Dekkema,
Melony Teague, Carol Ford,
Claudia Loopstra, and
Marguerite Cummings

JUDSON PRESS
PUBLISHERS SINCE 1824

Join our mailing list for updates and special offers.
www.judsonpress.com/mailing_list.cfm

Judson Press has made every effort to trace the ownership of all quotes. In the event of a question arising from the use of a quote, we regret any error made and will be pleased to make the necessary correction in future printings and editions of this book.

Melony Teague's photo used with permission by Karen Merk, www.merkphotography.com.
Claudia Loopstra's photo used with permission by Sarah Grace Photography, www.sarahgrace.ca.

Unless otherwise indicated, all Scriptures in this book are quoted from HOLY BIBLE, NEW INTERNATIONAL VERSION®. NIV®. Copyright © 1973, 1978, 1984, 2011 by Biblica, Inc.™ Used by permission. All rights reserved worldwide.

Scripture quotations marked (TNIV) are taken from the Holy Bible, Today's New International Version®. TNIV®. Copyright© 2001, 2005 by Biblica, Inc.™ Used by permission of Zondervan. All rights reserved worldwide. www.zondervan.com.

Interior design by Beth Oberholtzer.
Cover design by Wendy Ronga and Hampton Design Group.

Library of Congress Cataloging-in-Publication Data

Names: Dekkema, Glenda.
Title: As the ink flows : devotions to inspire christian writers & speakers / Glenda Dekkema, Melony Teague, Carol Ford, Claudia Loopstra, Marguerite Cummings.
Description: First [edition]. | Valley Forge : Judson Press, 2016. | Includes index.
Identifiers: LCCN 2015022227 | ISBN 9780817017675 (pbk. : alk. paper)
Subjects: LCSH: Authors—Prayers and devotions.
Classification: LCC BV4596.A85 A8 2016 | DDC 242/.68—dc23 LC record available at http://lccn.loc.gov/2015022227

Printed in the U.S.A.

First printing, 2016.

ADVANCE PRAISE FOR *AS THE INK FLOWS*

"This book elevates the craft of writing into a divine encounter where the author sits in the presence of God and allows the Holy Spirit, the most creative force in the universe, to speak to and through them. Let God speak to you through this book, then get to your keyboard!"

—Dr. Grant Mullen M.D., author of *Emotionally Free*

"*As the Ink Flows* is a dazzling goldmine of inspirational nuggets so creative and concise, it's a must-have devotional for writers, pastors, speakers, or *anyone* in ministry!"

—Julie Lessman, award-winning author of *The Daughters of Boston* and *Heart of San Francisco* series

"This book has reminded me that the joys and struggles I experience as a writer are the very means of grace toward that deepening intimacy. *As the Ink Flows* can easily be appreciated as a practical guide to incarnational living for those who have been created by God to write."

—Tracey-Ann Van Brenk M.Div., CSD Certified Spiritual Director, Guideposts Ministries

"Christians who suspect that writing could be something that they are called to do will find *As the Ink Flows* to be an answer to prayer."

—Bill Fledderus, senior editor of *Faith Today* and adjunct English instructor, Redeemer University College

"The authors of *As the Ink Flows* have prepared a real buffet of spiritual nourishment. Here are words to awaken and stir our creative impulses to continue our participation in God's redemptive story."

—Al Roberts, pastor, Calvary Baptist Church, Toronto

"Consistently inspiring, occasionally convicting, and refreshingly practical! It is my joy to recommend *As the Ink Flows* to writers who are passionate to see their written words reflect the immeasurably powerful and absolutely personal Living Word."

—Andy Frecka, author of *Winter Road*

"Too often writers focus on the words that they're putting on the page while neglecting the more important words that God is writing in their hearts. The authors bring together the two sides of the Christian writer's life—the study of craft and the study of the Word—in this thoughtful devotional."

—Jayne E. Self, Write! Canada Conference Director and author of Harbourlight's award-winning *Seaglass Mystery* series

"I believe that this powerful devotional will be of great value for those who want to honor God in everything they do."

—Paul Pascoal, pastor, Gormley Missionary Church, Ontario, and author of *Missões transculturais à porta de casa* (Cross-Cultural Missions at Your Front Door)

"This book inspired me with familiar ideas in a new context: have faith, take chances, trust in your calling at, of all places, my seemingly safe computer. I love how the questions for reflection create a conversational format—a wonderful way to invite the Holy Spirit to guide your creative spirit."

—Cameron Kaufman-Frey, pastor, Community Mennonite Church, Stouffville, Ontario

"Take the words of the best-selling book of all time, extrapolate examples of classic literary construct, and encourage writers of all kinds (songwriters, bloggers, pastors, and novelists) to recognize the living and moving presence and influence of the King of kings in their work."

—Suzy Weibel, co-author (with Dannah Gresh) of *Secret Diary Unlocked: My Struggle to Like Me* and *The One Year Devos for Teen Girls*

"I enjoyed the simple prayers, solidly biblical, practical advice, and nuggets of wisdom throughout this book. This book will simultaneously develop your writing skills and strengthen your faith in a sovereign God."

—Angela Reitsma Bick, editor of *Christian Courier*

To our families for their support,
to our friends for their feedback,
and to our association, The Word Guild—
for bringing us together and inspiring us.

"Our primary reason for creating The Word Guild in 2001 was to connect Canadian writers and editors who are Christian so that they could work together and help one another. I'm thrilled every time I see something like *As the Ink Flows*, which is not only a tangible example of writers supporting each other in Christian community, but also a means of reaching out to even more writers. What a great idea!"

—N. J. Lindquist, author and speaker, publisher of
the Hot Apple Cider Books, cofounder of The Word
Guild, and former director of Write! Canada

Contents

Introduction

As the Ink Flows tackles issues such as what it means to be a Christian writer, how to improve our craft, and what to do when the ink stops flowing onto the page. The five members of our local Christian writers' group ("Friends in The Word") offered support, ideas, prayer, editorial critique, and written contributions.

Each writer's unique literary style, struggles, and lessons learned have revealed themselves through this project in the same way an inkblot test uncovers hidden truths, motivations, or personality traits. We hope that the variety of voices, themes, and styles will speak to all our readers.

The layout of this book allows you to focus on God's Word and prayer for guidance in your writing, and it gives you an opportunity to practice the technique modeled in the chosen Scripture passages. The "Let the Ink Flow" pages provide the incentive to try something different and to be inspired and confident to use your God-given talents.

We have been blessed as individuals and as a group while writing this book, and it is our hope that you also will be strengthened, both spiritually and as writers, when you read and respond to its content.

Here are a few suggestions as to who could use this book.

Individual Writers. This book is intended for all Christian writers, journalists, and bloggers—from the amateur to the professional. If you want to begin the personal habit of journaling, the prompts for reflection and writing at the end of each devotion will provide a good starting point.

Small Groups. Whether your group is comprised of writers or you are gathered for Bible study, support, or a book study, we suggest that you open your meetings by reading one devotion. Another suggestion is to assign a "Let the Ink Flow" exercise to be shared at your next meeting.

Speakers. The devotions are intended to be inspirational to anyone who is at work furthering the kingdom of God. This includes but isn't limited to spiritual leaders, pastors, Christian teachers, songwriters, and educators. The questions and suggestions in "Let the Ink Flow" are designed to give additional insights into the Scriptures and your relationship to them, and to inspire you to use your God-given gifts.

As the Ink Flows (A Writer's Prayer)

Marguerite Cummings

As the ink flows
As the wind blows
May the words come easily
May I pray continually

> As the ink flows
> As my mind soars
> May your Word mold what I say
> May I serve you all the way

As the ink flows
As the work grows
May your love shine through and through
May my words glorify you

> As the ink flows
> As the fruit shows
> May we see your Kingdom come
> May you smile and say—
>   "Well done"

The Craft

Flow

Carol Ford

> But as for you, continue in what you have learned and have become convinced of, because you know those from whom you learned it, and how from infancy you have known the Holy Scriptures, which are able to make you wise for salvation through faith in Christ Jesus. All Scripture is God-breathed and is useful for teaching, rebuking, correcting and training in righteousness, so that the servant of God may be thoroughly equipped for every good work. (2 Timothy 3:14-17)

The term "flow,"[1] in recent years, is being used in business and education to describe an employee's or student's attitude. It's described as a state in which a person's performance exhibits full immersion, involvement, and enjoyment—an intrinsically rewarding feeling, one that balances a person's challenge with their skills and abilities to reach a goal—a feeling of competency.

Writers can definitely experience times of flow when ideas and words almost write themselves. We lose all track of time and all other distractions. Recently, as I lay awake in the early morning light, I mentally composed a compelling opening paragraph for a chapter in my book. I got up and quickly wrote the words. Within an astonishingly short period of time, the chapter unfolded. It was a wonderful and exciting event. I experienced flow.

Paul tells us in 2 Timothy 3:16, "All Scripture is God-breathed and is useful for teaching, rebuking, correcting and training in righteousness." What an amazing privilege for writers of the Bible; God held their pens and let them experience the flow.

As Christian writers, let's remember today where our "flow" originates.

PRAYER

Praise God, from whom all blessings flow;
Praise him, all creatures here below;
Praise him above, ye heavenly host;
Praise Father, Son, and Holy Ghost.[2] Amen.

Let the Ink Flow

When, if ever, have you experienced flow? What was the source of your inspiration? Use the framework of the Five W's (who, what, where, when, why) to describe your experiences in a paragraph or a poem.

PROMPT

List ways you can develop the flow of your writing moving forward.

NOTES

1. See Mihaly Csikszentmihalyi, *Finding Flow: The Psychology of Engagement with Everyday Life,* MasterMinds (New York: Basic Books, 1997).

2. Lyrics by Thomas Ken, 1674.

Give Thanks in All Circumstances

Glenda Dekkema

> Give thanks in all circumstances; for this is God's will for you in Christ Jesus. (1 Thessalonians 5:18)

This Bible passage reminds me of a scene from the film *The Hiding Place*, which is based on a true story about the German occupation of Holland during WWII. Corrie ten Boom and her sister, Betsie, are caught by the Nazis and sent to prison and later to a concentration camp as punishment for hiding and protecting Jews.

Shortly after arriving at the Ravensbrück camp, they are sent to their lice-infested barracks. Corrie nearly collapses. Betsie clasps her sister's hands and reminds her, "We are to give thanks in all circumstances." Corrie is incredulous, but prays anyway.

Soon the women learn that the guards won't enter the barracks because they are afraid of contracting the lice. The infestation becomes recognizable as a reason for giving thanks to God. The prisoners are free to talk, worship, and pray without any negative interference at the end of their long, laborious work days.

How does the biblical prescription "Give thanks in all circumstances" relate to your writing career? Have you ever received a rejection letter? If so, you're in very good company. Pearl Buck's *The Good Earth* was rejected fourteen times and went on to win the Pulitzer Prize.

What could happen to our writing careers if every time we received what seems like lice-infested feedback we prayed in all faith, "Thank you, Lord, for this"?

PRAYER

Lord, I thank you for any rejection letters and negative feedback. I don't know your purpose or your reasoning, but whatever it is, I accept it. Amen.

Let the Ink Flow

How do you deal with rejection? How might rejection be seen as a God-nudge toward sending material to the right markets, or taking a good, hard look at the quality of the material being submitted?

PROMPT

Write a prayer to the Lord in which you express your thoughts and feelings on this issue.

Writer's Block

Glenda Dekkema

> He says, "Be still, and know that I am God; I will be exalted among the nations, I will be exalted in the earth." (Psalm 46:10)

Roseanne Bane, in her book *Around the Writer's Block*, talks about our three major brain systems: the cortex, the limbic system, and the brain stem. She uses the metaphor of your body as a bus and your brain as a group of drivers "all jostling for the opportunity to get behind the wheel."[1] The cortex is the part of the brain that must be in the driver's seat if we are to think and work creatively. Our brain will allow us to use our creative center only if we are relaxed and at peace.

An ideal way for Christians to relax is by spending time in prayer or by spending time in spiritual retreat with God. Last fall I made one of the most profound decisions of my life. I was experiencing severe writer's block due to personal issues on the home front. I went solo to Cuba for one week with Christian books and my Bible packed in my suitcase. I did nothing other than read, pray, sit in silence, breathe deeply, journal, and pour out my heart to my Lord and Savior. I came into God's presence, and God responded by cradling me with an overwhelming sense of calmness, caring, and love. I was reminded of how many times the Bible tells us to "fear not." Ever since that vacation my heart, soul, and mind are at peace, and I am able to face what life is throwing at me. I am also able to write again.

PRAYER

Dear Lord, help me to be still and fully recognize that you are God and Lord, perfectly in control of this universe. Help me to come to you, be with you, and respond to you. Amen.

Let the Ink Flow

Describe your favorite ways in which you are able to be still and come into God's presence. You might want to take a couple of moments to be still before you do this.

PROMPT

Write an advice column on this topic.

NOTES

1. Roseanne Bane, *Around the Writer's Block: Using Brain Science to Solve Writer's Resistance* (New York: Penguin, 2012), 20.

Spit It Out

Melony Teague

> Let your gentleness be evident to all. The Lord is near. Do not be anxious about anything, but in every situation, by prayer and petition, with thanksgiving, present your requests to God. And the peace of God, which transcends all understanding, will guard your hearts and your minds in Christ Jesus. (Philippians 4:5-7)

For most, the least pleasant part of writing is when your editor takes out the red pen. We choose our words and craft our sentences to be succinct and interesting. We write and rewrite, edit and reedit, and then send it on for the dreaded editorial treatment.

Do you see God as your great editor when you come to God in the quiet moments of your day? Do you fear that God is critiquing your prayer requests or phrases as you pour out your heart? How much do you hold back for fear of saying the wrong thing, because we think it isn't proper to express ourselves without restraint, to our Almighty God?

Think of it this way: God, who loves us unconditionally, is not offended or intimidated by what you say or feel. God loves us. Now read John 3:16-17. There you go—now you have full freedom to come before God, through Jesus, to pour your heart out without fear. When you call on the Lord for help, God will not get upset with you or pull out a judgmental red pen.

Our God's mercies are new every morning. Who better to approach than the one who made you, who understands you, even when others don't seem to get your point? If you need to vent a little, God can take it. With petitioning and thanksgiving prayers, make your requests and emotions known to the Lord. You will receive some of the peace that "transcends all understanding."

PRAYER

Dear Jesus, what a relief to know that you have walked this earth before me. You know what it is like to be human. You love me through it all. Help me not to hold back, but to run always to you. Amen.

Let the Ink Flow

Think about how you feel when something is preying on your mind. How do you approach challenges? Examine the motives behind your knee-jerk reaction when you face criticism or critique.

PROMPT

Write God a heartfelt letter just as it comes out, straight onto the page. Resist the urge to edit it.

The Use of Metaphor

Claudia Loopstra

"You hypocrite, first take the plank out of your own eye, and then you will see clearly to remove the speck from the other person's eye."
(Matthew 7:5, TNIV)

Through the use of a plank as the metaphor for our own sin, and a speck as the metaphor for the sin of our fellow human beings, this illustration, employing exaggeration, creates a vivid comparison. We know enough not to take this literally, but if we visualize the size of a plank as compared to the dimensions of our eyes, it almost hurts to think about it. The example gives us a clear impression of the magnitude of the sin in our own lives; thus, it encourages us to examine that which needs to be taken care of before we begin to assist others in working on their comparatively tiny flaws.

Throughout his ministry Jesus uses metaphors as a teaching tool to make a point. In our own writing we are encouraged to use this technique to make a distinct impression so that our readers can understand the message that we hope to convey.

PRAYER

Lord God, I praise you for the way in which you teach me many things through your Word. Help me to glorify you with clarity as I write my stories. May I be a megaphone proclaiming you from the rooftops. Amen.

Let the Ink Flow

Reflect on the best metaphors that you may have used in your own work. Why did you use them?

PROMPT

Using the theme of how we ought to look at our own sin before looking at another's, write your own metaphor.

Ten Thousand Hours

Glenda Dekkema

> Yet you, LORD, are our Father. We are the clay, you are the potter; we are all the work of your hand. (Isaiah 64:8)

Neither Zondervan nor InterVarsity nor Judson Press will knock on your door with flowers and a check as soon as they read your fledgling attempts at writing—despite how gifted you are. I believe that God has put the desire in my heart to be a writer. Because you are reading this devotional for writers, I assume that God has also given you this ambition. If God is the potter and we are the clay, then it only makes sense that the Lord must have also given us the talents to fulfill these aspirations.

God gave us the raw ability, but God asks us to work diligently at improving our craft. In Malcolm Gladwell's book *Outliers: The Story of Success*, the author says that the phrase "overnight success" is a myth. Those who become truly accomplished reach this status only after putting in about ten thousand hours of practice. I tell my children this when they complain about practicing the piano, but it doesn't go over very well. Can you picture them rolling their eyes? However, if we love what we do, we can appreciate this advice.

Romans 12:6-7 says, "We have different gifts, according to the grace given to each of us. If your gift is prophesying, then prophesy in accordance with your faith; if it is serving, then serve; if it is teaching, then teach." And let me add, if it is writing, then write!

PRAYER

Thank you, Lord, for putting the desire in my heart to write. Thank you for giving me this precious gift to fulfill your purposes. Help me to continue to work at my talents until they are pleasing to you. Amen.

Let the Ink Flow

Go back in time; think honestly about how many hours you have devoted to writing. Include all your time working, reading, researching, and taking courses. Once you have added up all the time you have spent learning the craft of writing, come back and write your thoughts here. How close are you to ten thousand hours?

PROMPT

Write out one thousand words for a first draft only. Time how long it takes.

Repetition

Carol Ford

> The wicked desire the plunder of evildoers, but the root of the righteous flourishes. Evildoers are trapped by their sinful talk, and so the innocent escape trouble. From the fruit of their lips people are filled with good things, and the work of their hands brings them reward. (Proverbs 12:12-14, TNIV)

The repeated structure in this Scripture passage brings rhythm, emphasis, and momentum to the writer's topic. The technical term for this poetic type of repetition or parallelism is isocolon.[1] It's a technique commonly found in Hebrew poetry—and in Jesus' teaching.

I try to avoid repeating the same word in my writing and strive to vary sentence structure. However, repetition can be very effective when used sparingly. Jesus used the repetitive style of Hebrew poetry when he spoke the Beatitudes: "Blessed are the poor in spirit. . . . Blessed are those who mourn. . . . Blessed are the meek. . . . Blessed are those who hunger and thirst for righteousness. . . . Blessed are the merciful. . . . Blessed are the pure in heart. . . . Blessed are the peacemakers. . . . Blessed are those who are persecuted because of righteousness" (Matthew 5:3-11).

Let's read today's Scripture passages and bask not only in the beauty of their style, but also in the way they can strengthen our Christian walk.

PRAYER

Lord, I thank you for your written word and ask for your blessings today as I practice new skills. Amen.

Let the Ink Flow

Do you hesitate to embrace this technique of repetition? If so, why? What might be the benefits of such a tool?

PROMPT

Practice using the writing technique of isocolon to describe an event in your life—for example, a loss, an exciting time, or a character in your book.

NOTES

1. "Isocolon is a type of communication that includes separate parts that complement each other with similar lengths, styles, or meanings. Words or phrases in isocolon may have the same numbers of syllables, be based on the same root words, or otherwise provide what's called parallelism. Parallelism and other rhetorical methods give a longer phrase or sentence more of a defined and comprehensive pattern" (http://www.wisegeek.com/what-is-an-isocolon.htm).

Opposites Attract

Carol Ford

> Better a little with the fear of the LORD than great wealth with turmoil.
> Better a small serving of vegetables with love than a fattened calf
> with hatred. (Proverbs 15:16-17)

This Scripture reading points out what is really important in our lives; it's not wealth or riches, but a healthy fear of the Lord, having contentment and loving relationships.

The book of Proverbs is full of rich and thoughtful guidelines for living. Solomon's writing style uses compact, contrasting statements to express truth about human nature. Proverbs 28:2 says, "When a country is rebellious, it has many rulers, but a ruler with discernment and knowledge maintains order." Verse 4 continues on a similar theme, observing, "Those who forsake instruction praise the wicked, but those who heed it resist them."

As a reader, I tend to stop and reflect on comparison statements. It can be an excellent writing technique to evoke reader response. You may want to try this style for an article or editorial piece.

PRAYER

Lord, help me to see the Bible as your guidebook for my life. I ask you today to bless and inspire my writing in a fresh way. Amen.

Let the Ink Flow

How has God used opposites in your life to get your attention?

Practice writing a few contrast statements using some of the following antonyms:

intentional/ accidental	accept/refuse	beginning/end	peace/war
join/separate	bend/straighten	teacher/pupil	tight/slack
junior/senior	rigid/pliable	thick/thin	east/west
night/day	rough/smooth	internal/external	slow/fast
new/old	victory/defeat	near/far	hard/easy
north/south	top/bottom	wet/dry	supply/demand
past/present	virtue/vice	noisy/quiet	beautiful/ugly

Motivated to Journal

Claudia Loopstra

> My son, keep my words and store up my commands within you. Keep my commands and you will live; guard my teachings as the apple of your eye. Bind them on your fingers; write them on the tablet of your heart. (Proverbs 7:1-3)

When my grandmother passed away in 1965, I became the beneficiary of a diary she had received as a Christmas gift from her two daughters in 1933. Frustrated by the skimpy amount of information gleaned from her musings, I craved more detail. With Grandma's passing, there would no longer be the opportunity.

This little book gave me the impetus for journaling. In 1985 I experienced a Road to Damascus encounter with Jesus Christ. It was a life-changing event that redirected my focus. I stepped up my journaling. By doing this, I was able to gather information that chronicled the extraordinary way God had been working in my life.

As I continue to write my memoir, I have learned the value of recording my life story. So many things I had forgotten—important things that need to be told. I think of my six grandchildren and the legacy I intend to leave with respect to my coming to saving faith in Jesus Christ.

Often, we include Scripture references in our writing. When we have made it a practice to know where Scripture verses are located, we have a tendency to turn quickly to the passage. In that way, it may be said that it has been written on the tablets of our hearts. This is a metaphor for remembering, that which has been taught to us by God.

God underscores the importance of remembering his words. As we document our journals, may we find the nuggets in our stories that may help others as they journey through life.

PRAYER

Thank you, Lord, for helping me write about the important details of my life. Please continue to nurture me in my faith and spiritual growth. Amen.

Let the Ink Flow

In your own life, what method have you used to remember details that you plan to write about?

PROMPT

It's been said it takes twenty-one days to form a habit. Take up the challenge and begin journaling tomorrow. (I have to give you time to buy your journal!) Prayerfully give this over to God. After twenty-one days, look back and see how God has worked in your life—what the Spirit has revealed to you. How have you felt God's presence? Have prayers been answered? Are you waiting on God for something in particular? Has God been with you through a difficult time?

Libel

Glenda Dekkema

> The mouths of fools are their undoing, and their lips are a snare to their very lives. The words of a gossip are like choice morsels; they go down to the inmost parts. (Proverbs 18:7-8)

The law of the land says that you can write and publish whatever you want about a person, even if it ruins their reputation, as long as it is *true*. I know I often fall into the temptation to gossip. Whenever I do, I feel worse about myself. Fortunately, it is easier to delete gossip from writing than from the spoken word because we have enough time to go back and edit.

"Libel" is the legal term used for published allegations or misrepresentations. But the law of the land is not the higher being to whom we as Christians must answer. We ought to examine our own hearts and consider our motivations before making the decision to write about others.

Romans 2:1 says, "You, therefore, have no excuse, you who pass judgment on someone else, for at whatever point you judge another, you are condemning yourself, because you who pass judgment do the same things."

The gift of writing—when used with or without wisdom—is indeed mightier than the sword.

PRAYER

Dear Lord, help me to use wisdom if and when I consider writing negatively about others. If I am motivated by jealousy, inappropriate zeal, or other emotions that do not serve you well, please stop the action of both my tongue and my pen. Amen.

Let the Ink Flow

Think about someone you don't like. Why don't you like this person? Does your dislike of that person tell you anything about yourself?

PROMPT

Write a full description of the good qualities of this person: motivation, favorite sayings, greatest fears and loves. Whom does he or she admire? If you don't know the answer to these questions, consider asking the person.

Be the Media

Glenda Dekkema

> Woe to those who call evil good and good evil, who put darkness for
> light and light for darkness, who put bitter for sweet and sweet for bitter.
> (Isaiah 5:20)

Over the past few years, I have been examining the misinformation portrayed in the mainstream media. Usually this deliberate distortion of the truth has an evil goal: sell at all costs even if it is damaging to human health, animals, or the earth; highlight war as the best/only option for obtaining peace, glamorize debauchery to normalize sin.

As a registered nurse, I am particularly concerned about the misinformation regarding health care for the purposes of profit, particularly in the pharmaceutical industry. It isn't appropriate in this devotional to go into the nitty-gritty details of these lies, but I will say that it's easy for money to motivate people to do horrendous things. As it says in 1 Timothy 6:10, "For the love of money is the root of all kinds of evil." Many prominent individuals are struggling to uncover truths, and they are being ridiculed or harmed by the powers that be. I have a duty to listen to what the truthseekers have to say—no matter how unpleasant it is to hear—and only then should I make a decision as to what to believe and write.

Let's do our research. Use due diligence. Write into the light.

PRAYER

Lord, help me to be the light in this world through my writing. May you open my eyes to hidden truths. Amen.

Let the Ink Flow

Think about two or three lies viewed through the mainstream media that you find particularly unjust. Why?

Do you believe that you have a mission to right the wrong? If so, write a letter to the editor of your local newspaper on an issue close to your heart.

Lyrics

Glenda Dekkema

> At that very time Jesus cured many who had diseases, sicknesses
> and evil spirits, and gave sight to many who were blind. So he replied to
> the messengers, "Go back and report to John what you have seen and
> heard: The blind receive sight, the lame walk, those who have leprosy
> are cleansed, the deaf hear, the dead are raised, and the good news
> is proclaimed to the poor. Blessed is anyone who does not stumble on
> account of me." (Luke 7:21-23)

Bryan Moyer Suderman is a Christian songwriter and performer of songs of faith for all ages. The following song shows how the Scriptures can be turned into palpable and vivid words for today's world. Isn't that what we, as Christian writers, are trying to do? Let's spend time with the gospel, and get to know it deeply so that our words inspire others, whether in spiritual songs, poems, fiction, or nonfiction. Let's get our inspiration from the greatest book of all time.

"Detectives of Divinity"
We are detectives of divinity; we're looking all around
For signs of God's activity wherever they are found.
God is up to something, of that we can be sure;
So start the investigation, the clues are everywhere.[1]

PRAYER

Beloved God, we know that "you are up to something." Help us to clearly see your activity and then help us to write the words that will inspire others. Amen.

Let the Ink Flow

Jot down fifty places where you see God's activity.

Choose the best ones and then write a poem or song lyrics about them.

1. Bryan Moyer Suderman, *Detectives of Divinity: Songs of Faith for Small and Tall* (Small Tall Music, 2011). Used by permission.

The Hook

Carol Ford

> In the beginning was the Word, and the Word was with God, and the
> Word was God. He was with God in the beginning. Through him all
> things were made; without him nothing was made that has been made.
> In him was life, and that life was the light of all people. The light shines
> in the darkness, and the darkness has not overcome it. (John 1:1-5, TNIV)

John's opening line mirrors Genesis 1:1, "In the beginning. . . ." He takes us right back to when God spoke the world into being. John then tells us that "the Word was with God, and the Word was God. He was with God in the beginning." What does this mean? He refers to the Word as a person and foreshadows what the arrival of the Word will mean to humankind—light in the darkness.

Are these opening sentences a good hook for John's Gospel? Effective hooks make us want to read more, ask questions, reveal main characters, involve us emotionally, and hint at problems or conflicts. I believe that John has met these criteria.

Because I am currently writing my own life story, I've been reading a variety of other memoirs to observe opening lines. Jeannette Walls's memoir *The Glass Castle* begins this way: "I was sitting in a taxi, wondering if I had overdressed for the evening, when I looked out the window and saw Mom rooting through a Dumpster."[1] This sentence stirred my interest and curiosity immediately.

Another author, Carolyn Weber, opens her book *Surprised by Oxford* with this line: "My arrival in Oxford, England, that early October of 1994 came with plenty of baggage."[2] Carolyn packed the essence of her book into only fifteen words—location, time, and a play on the word "baggage."

It is my desire to emulate these successful authors.

PRAYER

Lord, let me write compelling and unique content that will honor you and be shared with others. Amen.

Let the Ink Flow

REFLECTION

Think about your favorite opening lines. What draws your attention to them?

PROMPT

Write a couple of opening sentences about a common theme and include all the good elements of an effective hook. Example topics: Christmas, wedding day, vacation.

NOTES

1. Jeannette Walls, *The Glass Castle: A Memoir* (New York: Scribner, 2005), 3.
2. Carolyn Weber, *Surprised by Oxford: A Memoir* (Nashville: Thomas Nelson, 2011), 11.

A Different Perspective

Melony Teague

> And he died for all, that those who live should no longer live for them-
> selves but for him who died for them and was raised again. So from
> now on we regard no one from a worldly point of view. Though we once
> regarded Christ in this way, we do so no longer. Therefore, if anyone is
> in Christ, the new creation has come: The old has gone, the new is here!
> (2 Corinthians 5:15-17)

You know the importance of a "point of view" within a story, an article, or a manuscript. So also, in life, the challenge is to see life through someone else's perspective. Perhaps it would be good to think about these events from the point of view of the prodigal son, or the woman at the well, or even dear, doubting Thomas. Perhaps in understanding these biblical characters we can better understand those around us too.

I challenge you to see life events through new eyes. This may in-volve putting aside all your preconceived ideas and being open to seeing them in a new light. In 2 Corinthians 5:16, Paul talks about "a worldly point of view." It is probably the easiest point of view to fall into. But we can choose to take a careful look and see the heavenly perspective as well as the point of view of others who may be observing us.

As your life story with Jesus unfolds each day, be aware of its testimony—your very powerful and precious "point of view."

PRAYER

Dear Jesus, help me to see annual Christian celebrations from your point of view. May I be aware of others' perspectives so I can be an instrument of grace, love, and understanding to help them see your perspective on life. Thank you for helping me to put aside my pre-conceived ideas so I can be open to seeing my Christian life through your eyes, and my testimony will be one that pleases. Amen.

Let the Ink Flow

What are some ways you might learn to see things from a different perspective?

Think of a favorite piece of writing and rewrite it from another character's point of view, or if you prefer, rewrite it in a different genre or time period. Then, choose a Bible story and rewrite it from another point of view or in a genre that you like (contemporary, historical, or futuristic).

Literary Critique

Glenda Dekkema

> Coming to his hometown, he began teaching the people in their syn-
> agogue, and they were amazed. "Where did this man get this wisdom
> and these miraculous powers?" they asked. "Isn't this the carpenter's
> son? Isn't his mother's name Mary, and aren't his brothers James,
> Joseph, Simon and Judas? Aren't all his sisters with us? Where then
> did this man get all these things?" And they took offense at him. But
> Jesus said to them, "A prophet is not without honor except in his own
> town and in his own home." (Matthew 13:54-57)

If you are fortunate enough to have siblings, then probably you have experienced from an early age what it is like to be teased, taunted, and criticized—in addition to all the fun, of course. This is excellent preparation for a writing career that inevitably involves rejection letters, editorial critique, and literary reviews—in addition to all the fun, of course.

When one of my loved ones praises my work, it can feel like an obligatory compliment offered to make me feel better. However, when a stranger praises me, it sounds like celebratory trumpets.

What about criticism? Is there a difference there as well? Does a stranger's criticism hurt less because "They don't really get it!" or "What do they know anyway?" Does a loved one's criticism hurt more because "They're supposed to support me"?

This passage in the book of Matthew shows that Jesus understands the need to get out of our familiar circles to reach a different audience. We shouldn't let our loved ones' criticism demolish our dreams, nor allow their praise prevent us from assiduously developing our talents.

Imagine the result if Jesus had become discouraged by the people in his hometown and had never gone to other places to spread the word of the gospel.

PRAYER

Lord, please continue to give me the courage I need. Amen.

Let the Ink Flow

List your greatest supporters. What is their relationship to you? Then list your worst critics and their relationship to you.

PROMPT

Examine these two lists and write thank-you notes to those who have encouraged you the most.

Your Soundtrack

Melony Teague

> Let the message of Christ dwell among you richly as you teach and admonish one another with all wisdom through psalms, hymns, and songs from the Spirit, singing to God with gratitude in your hearts. (Colossians 3:16)

If you watch a movie on DVD and view the deleted scenes, without the soundtrack, you will notice the difference that music makes. Similarly, if you like to have music playing while you write, you know that the kind of music you listen to while writing can have a profound effect on your work. Music captures or arouses emotion. It can be a catalyst to loosen the tongue and inspire the heart. Music seems to be the backdrop to life and love. It sets the mood, whether joyful, romantic, or sombre.

If you were to pick a playlist for your day, what would it be? Think carefully, since the songs you pick will set the tone. Do you have a theme song for your life right now? Is there one that encourages your heart?

It has become popular for authors to share their playlists with their readers. Have you thought about sharing yours?

PRAYER

Dear Jesus, fill my heart with songs daily. Please grant me a joyful, uplifting soundtrack so I can always share your joy. Amen.

Let the Ink Flow

Write down some songs that have meant something to you in your life. What pattern or theme seems to emerge? Is it one that you want to keep singing, or do you sense a need for a remix?

Write about what God is showing you through this exercise.

Writers' Groups

Glenda Dekkema

> Be devoted to one another in love. Honor one another above yourselves.
> (Romans 12:10)

Something was missing from the writers' groups I have belonged to in the past. It was only after I started attending The Word Guild and found other Christian writers willing to be part of a group that I found my paper, ink, and soul haven.

Writers' groups typically offer support and critique to their members. The writers may commend each other for the act of writing, for keeping the pace, and for sending out their writing for publication. They may also submit material on a rotational basis to group members for earned praise and delicate criticism.

I believe that our group has managed to successfully combine support and feedback. More importantly, we have a third powerful element that's absent in the other writers' groups I've mentioned. We open with devotion and close with prayer requests. During the weeks between our meetings, we pray for each other. We may ask for strength to pursue a particular publishing option, confidence to keep writing, or help with some personal matter unrelated to writing.

God tells us in Romans 12:10 to "be devoted to one another" and to "honor one another." By doing as we are commanded, we will all benefit in our writing careers.

PRAYER

Dear Lord, may I find and cherish the Christian support I need from individuals or in a group. Please be at the center of our discussions. Amen.

Let the Ink Flow

Are you part of a writers' group? Why or why not?

PROMPT

Take the steps necessary today to connect with fellow writers. Use online resources if you need to find a good fit.

Write Your Own Parable

Melony Teague

> The disciples came to him and asked, "Why do you speak to the people in parables?" He replied, "Because the knowledge of the secrets of the kingdom of heaven has been given to you, but not to them. Whoever has will be given more, and they will have an abundance. Whoever does not have, even what they have will be taken from them. This is why I speak to them in parables: Though seeing, they do not see; though hearing, they do not hear or understand." (Matthew 13:10-13)

Jesus used parables to teach the disciples and others. Parables tell a story in such a way that the meaning is hidden but can be discovered upon further investigation. It is a way of teaching those who will understand without divulging the true meaning to those who would misinterpret or despise it. Parables can be used to hide truth until the proper time in which it is to be revealed.

The disciples didn't always like Jesus' approach. Perhaps they wanted to have it all worked out for them. When we put pen to paper, do we always lay it all out there? Is there perhaps a time to use the parable method to encourage readers to investigate more deeply on their own?

In my experience, a truth that is sought out, discovered, and carefully uncovered becomes one that belongs to the finder of the truth. It becomes all the more precious when we finally understand it.

PRAYER

Dear Jesus, may I always have my heart and ears open to receive truths that you give. May I always be willing to search out those nuggets of truth and share them, even if they take a little bit of foraging to find. Amen.

Let the Ink Flow

What is it about parables that stand out as a lesson to you?

Write your own modern-day parable illustrating a life lesson.

Journal Writer

Glenda Dekkema

Listen to my words, LORD, consider my lament. Hear my cry for help, my King and my God, for to you I pray. In the morning, LORD, you hear my voice; in the morning I lay my requests before you and wait expectantly. (Psalm 5:1-3)

The book of Psalms gives us a remarkable example of the range of emotions in human spirituality. David and the other psalmists shared their deepest thoughts, fears, anguish, and praise.

For many writers, this is commonly done through journal writing. However, unlike in the psalms, which were compiled for corporate worship, the intention of journal writing is for one's own purpose. The privacy of the journal allows writers to bare their souls.

My sister, Teresa Veltman, has kept a prayer journal over the past twenty years. I've never seen it, of course, because it is private, but I'm curious! She has said, "When I go back through my prayer journal, I see that the God of the universe, responsible for the whole world and everyone in it, bothers to take my concerns seriously. My little life is important enough for God to answer my prayers. There are many times I have simply forgotten what I prayed about until I reread my earlier entries. Sometimes it has taken months or years for my prayers to be answered."

A journal can be a powerful agent in helping us to focus our lives, set goals, and make prayer requests. Besides that, it's a great writing tool. I am keeping a daily journal in which I write only a few lines a day. I have already noticed how God is working in my life. You too may wish to periodically return to your journal to see God's wonderful and miraculous ways.

PRAYER

Lord, thank you for listening to all of my concerns. You are the great and mighty Lord, and yet you take seriously all the little issues of my life. Thank you, Lord, for your attention to detail. Thank you for caring. Amen.

Let the Ink Flow

Journal writing doesn't necessarily have to be done every day, which is different from the expectation of writing daily in a diary. A journal can have the sole purpose of writing down thoughts and prayers, when and as they come, that you would like to bring to the Lord.

PROMPT

If you have a unique journal that you keep, or if your journal has meant something special to you, please write about it here. If you don't have a journal yet, describe the kind of journal you'd like to have. If possible, tell why you want it to be as described.

Setting the Scene

Melony Teague

> Above the vault over their heads was what looked like a throne of lapis lazuli, and high above on the throne was a figure like that of a man. I saw that from what appeared to be his waist up he looked like glowing metal, as if full of fire, and that from there down he looked like fire; and brilliant light surrounded him. Like the appearance of a rainbow in the clouds on a rainy day, so was the radiance around him. (Ezekiel 1:26-28a)

In the first verses of Ezekiel 1 we see how the scene has been carefully set for one of the most mind-blowing visions where Ezekiel is appointed and sent to Israel. We are told the exact date, who the king was, and exactly where Ezekiel was, who his father was, and who was with Ezekiel at the time (Ezekiel 1:1-3). In verses 26-28a the writer did an efficient job in preparing the way for the entrance of the one who speaks to him.

If you were to look at your own life in the same way, how has the scene been set for God to show up? How can you better clarify your own very special, unique purpose on earth? How can you convey the message that you have been given and pass it on through your writing? How comfortable are you with the awareness that this is your privilege and purpose as a Christian writer? Set the scene in your own life today to welcome the coming of God's message to you through the Word.

PRAYER

Dear Jesus, I want you to show up in my life. Help me to set the scene so that you have the freedom to use me as you will. Amen.

Let the Ink Flow

Think about the questions posed in today's devotion. Examine your heart. What fears do you have connected with setting the scene for God to show up?

How can you intentionally set the scene for God to work in your life today?

Show, Don't Tell

Glenda Dekkema

In the temple courts he found people selling cattle, sheep and doves,
and others sitting at tables exchanging money. So he made a whip out
of cords, and drove all from the temple courts, both sheep and cattle;
he scattered the coins of the moneychangers and overturned their
tables. To those who sold doves he said, "Get these out of here! Stop
turning my Father's house into a market!" (John 2:14-16)

Most writing courses will teach you, "Show, don't tell." I found that
this was one of the most difficult lessons to learn. We need to slow
down and write about something that we want to highlight by showing (as in John 2:14-16) and then telling (see John 2:23) to bring us
to the next event.

We have a wonderful example of "Show, don't tell" in this passage from John's Gospel. John could have said, "Jesus was angry
because people were misusing the holy temple by turning the place of
worship into a market for money making." Telling the story in this
way still would have been accurate, but far less effective.

John, without the benefit of any writing course, used the elements
of "Show, don't tell" through dialogue, sensory language, and detail.
Through dialogue John showed that Jesus was angry: "Get these out
of here! Stop turning my Father's house into a market!" Through
sensory language he showed what Jesus had done: "he scattered the
coins of the moneychangers and overturned the tables." It's easy to
visualize the anger powering this action.

Sometimes I am hesitant to "show" in my writing what I truly feel
because doing so makes me vulnerable to criticism. But "showing" is
far more effective with readers because it draws them into the emotions as well as the struggles.

PRAYER

Lord, thank you for showing us Jesus as truly human and truly God
at the same time. Amen.

Let the Ink Flow

Look for another example where the Scriptures have effectively used the "Show, don't tell" principle.

PROMPT

Use a recent piece of your writing and rewrite it with the intention to enhance it by using this technique. Don't be afraid to exaggerate and expand your work past your comfort zone.

Learning Discipline through Blogging

Melony Teague

Each of you should use whatever gift you have received to serve others, as faithful stewards of God's grace in its various forms. (1 Peter 4:10)

I started my writing career as a blogger. Each day when I got up, my routine included a daily blog. At first this was a personal search for my best health, nutrition, and fitness. It instilled in me the valuable habit of being disciplined enough to write daily. As I continued, my blogging expanded to a more public platform and I learned to be a good steward of the writing gifts I have been given by remaining faithful to the task.

I cannot overestimate the value that blogging has added to my writing. I write in a different style, one that is less formal and more conversational. I took photos of food and posted them online and encouraged others to seek a healthier way of life, so that they can look after the bodies given to them for this earthly experience. Whether I am sharing recipes or life's truths gleaned from the school of hard knocks (and more recently I have added book reviews), I still blog daily. I have a global following. I would never have met these precious people apart from the avenue of my blog.

If you do not yet blog, how could you use blogging as a way to reach others through the web? In what ways could you use it as a tool not only to help instill self-discipline in your own writing but also to encourage and uplift others?

PRAYER

Lord, help me to be aware of ways I might be more disciplined in order to be a better steward of the gifts you have given me. For your glory, show me ways I might grow as a writer in creativity and in self-discipline. Amen.

Let the Ink Flow

When you apply 1 Peter 4:10 to your writing, how do you think that being more self-disciplined might benefit you?

Do you blog? If not, consider creating a blog as a form of self-discipline in your writing life. If you do already have a blog, how can you better use it as a tool to establish the habit of writing daily?

Hand in Hand

Melony Teague

> After Jesus had finished instructing his twelve disciples, he went on from there to teach and preach in the towns of Galilee. When John, who was in prison, heard about the deeds of the Messiah, he sent his disciples to ask him, "Are you the one who is to come, or should we expect someone else?" (Matthew 11:1-3)

John the Baptist had disciples who followed him. Jesus was the model of how to disciple. He taught his chosen followers so that they, in turn, would know how to make disciples once the appropriate time came to "go and make disciples of all nations" (see Matthew 28). I often wonder what it must have been like for the disciples to have Jesus as their physical teacher on this earth. To their credit, the disciples went and did as Jesus had instructed them (Matthew 21:6).

As we grow as Christians, it is important to be a disciple and to disciple others. Staying the same can bring us into an unimpassioned, possibly passive, relationship with our Lord.

Discipleship and mentoring go hand in hand. In your journey as a writer, there are those who undoubtedly will benefit from your mentoring. Consider sharing your gifts and insight with someone else. Are you willing to take the hands of less-experienced writers to guide them toward being good stewards of the gifts they have been given? Our acts of discipleship and mentoring will not be unsupported; we have a wonderful promise that Jesus, our mentor, is with us always, to the very end (Matthew 28:20).

PRAYER

Dear Jesus, as I think about mentoring and discipleship, lead me and guide me. I want to be your disciple and bring others into discipleship with you. Help me to be the best disciple and mentor I can be, for your glory. Amen.

Let the Ink Flow

Think and pray about persons you can influence, both in their writing and in their Christian growth.

PROMPT

When has someone extended a helping hand to you as a writer? What was your response? Consider how to thank them for their support.

The Divine Word

Glenda Dekkema

> For prophecy never had its origin in the human will, but prophets, though human, spoke from God as if they were carried along by the Holy Spirit.
> (2 Peter 1:21)

God is revealed to people in the Bible through prophets, angels, plagues, dreams, stars, and even a baby leaping in the womb—to name a few. In the story of the burning bush, we read that God speaks directly with Moses. The Bible is a profound, hermetic collection of books that has inspired and challenged scholars and non-scholars alike throughout the ages.

The Bible was written without the benefit of paper, ballpoint pen, eraser, computer, spellcheck, thesaurus, writers' groups or conferences, printing press—or coffee. Yet it continues to dramatically change hearts and lives. How can that be? I believe that the answer lies in the power of God's Holy Spirit.

The Bible is a whole library containing all the elements of great writing, such as suspense, dialogue, voice, point of view, poetry, truth, drama, insight, metaphors and analogies, short stories, and setting. There is only one response to the magnificence of this living Word: it is divinely inspired.

PRAYER

Dear Lord, I know that your Word is divine and infallible. I am humbled by your greatness. Amen.

Let the Ink Flow

One suggestion often made in writing courses is to imitate the style of great works of literature. Do you see the benefit in doing this? Why or why not?

Choose three Bible passages with different writing styles. How do you relate to each style? Where do you see the divine in the passages you have chosen?

Inspiration

Evergreen

Carol Ford

> The king again asked, "Queen Esther, what is your petition? It will be
> given you. What is your request? Even up to half the kingdom, it will be
> granted." Then Queen Esther answered, "If I have found favor with you,
> Your Majesty, and if it pleases you, grant me my life—this is my petition.
> And spare my people—this is my request." (Esther 7:2b-3)

We never seem to tire of stories like Esther—with a hero, often from
an underprivileged background, a villain, suspense, a climax, and
God's provision in desperate situations. What drama! Writing such
as this, considered to be sustainable and lasting and relevant long
past its publication, is referred to as "evergreen content."

Another example of a timeless plot is the exciting story of Daniel's
refusal to change his convictions, his testing in the lions' den, and
God's intervention to save his life (read Daniel 6). A writer could use
this storyline to develop a children's book to show courage for standing up for what is right, even though it is not popular (e.g., speaking
up when friends are bullied).

The story of David's infidelity with Bathsheba in 2 Samuel 11:2-4,
describing how he let his lustful thoughts lead him into a sinful relationship, definitely qualifies as evergreen content. David is told by his
messenger, "She is Bathsheba, the daughter of Eliam and the wife of
Uriah the Hittite." Then David sent messengers to get her. There is
no shortage of this type of temptation in our current society and the
consequences that it produces.

This is just a small sample of the many stories in the Scriptures
that could provide prompts for our own writing. Let's be creative
and find new ways to help our readers know that what once was old
is new again.

PRAYER

Lord, please help me to write content that will attract readers to my
blog, articles, and other publications that share a Christian world-
view on topics that never go out of style. Amen.

Let the Ink Flow

Examples of subjects that never get old are love and romance, food, finance/saving money, parenting, jobs and careers, and pets. Formats might include lists, top tips, instructional "how-to" tutorials, and book reviews. If this concept is new to you, take time to do an Internet search on "evergreen content."

Try writing an article on one of the suggested subjects using a sample format listed above. For example, you might write on "10 Tips for Christians Who Use Internet Dating Sites." Consider submitting the article to a local newspaper or Christian publication.

Where Are You Looking?

Melony Teague

> The LORD said to Moses, "Send some men to explore the land of Canaan, which I am giving to the Israelites. From each ancestral tribe send one of its leaders." . . . "We seemed like grasshoppers in our own eyes, and we looked the same to them." (Numbers 13:1-2,33a)

How we see ourselves can affect our ability to inherit what God has promised. When the people had a "grasshopper" self-image, they felt inferior, threatened, discouraged, and possibly outnumbered. They were so close to the fulfillment of God's promise and they missed out. They grumbled and rebelled against God and they saw themselves as insignificant.

Not much has changed over the millennia; we still fall into the trap of doubting what God has promised. We might compare ourselves to others causing us to feel inferior, especially nowadays when social media puts our lives on public display. We limit what God can do through us. Sometimes it is not our "out-look" that needs changing, but our "in-look," so that we can move forward with what God has given us to do. What I mean is, when we look within ourselves, do we see what God has made out of us—a holy people and a royal priesthood who have a great God on our side? This is not because of our own superiority but because of what has been done for us through the cross of Calvary. Are we comparing ourselves to others in our "out-look"? As long as we keep in mind whose we are, there is no room for a "grasshopper" mentality.

We are children of the almighty God, who have been given our own unique gifts to use for God's glory.

PRAYER

Dear Jesus, help me to realize that you see me with eyes of tremendous love and grace. Help me to have a healthy "in-look." As I trust in you, please bring forth in me what you have promised. Thank you for always being with me. Amen.

Let the Ink Flow

Identify some "grasshopper" mentality traits in yourself, and bring them to the Lord in prayer.

Take a moment to examine your own "in-look." Does it need to be adjusted to align with how God sees you? How have wounds from the words of others hindered you in seeing yourself through your Savior's eyes? Write about it in a letter to God, or if you prefer, in a poem.

Taken Your Temperature Lately?

Melony Teague

> I know your deeds, that you are neither cold nor hot. I wish you were either one or the other! So, because you are lukewarm—neither hot nor cold—I am about to spit you out of my mouth. You say, "I am rich; I have acquired wealth and do not need a thing." But you do not realize that you are wretched, pitiful, poor, blind and naked. (Revelation 3:15-17)

Do you remember when you saw your first published work in print? Did you show it to everyone who would pay attention? Perhaps you were a little more discreet in showing your excitement. Either way, you must have felt proud. You may have felt as if you could conquer the world. In a way, those feelings of euphoria were part of the excitement that you felt, a kind of "first love" and passion for writing, if you will. It reminds me of being "hot," as in the Revelation text, and how we should strive to maintain that same passion about our writing, and definitely not become "lukewarm," lacking inspiration, purpose, and vision.

Those who have been writing for a while may feel like the honeymoon is over, particularly when dealing with multiple rewrites or struggling to meet a deadline. Just as we are to guard our hearts against losing our first love for the Lord in our spiritual journey, the same principle may apply to our first love for writing. Take a moment to examine your own writing "temperature"—are you on fire? When the signs of lukewarm words show up on the page, take a step back and prayerfully find your passion again; your words will be revived, and your writing will once again become invigorated, and inspiring. The best advice may be: "Do the things you did at first" (Revelation 2:5).

PRAYER

Dear Jesus, I know that in much the same way as I guard my heart against becoming lukewarm, I need to keep an eye on my writing temperature. Breathe new life into all I do. Amen.

Let the Ink Flow

Ever had one of those "blah" writing days when you really have no inspiration? How did you move through it?

If you are feeling uninspired, think of ways you can rekindle your passion for writing. Document a time when you were ablaze with inspiration and passion for what you write to encourage others, and let this serve as a reminder to yourself when that passion seems to be waning.

When Thunder Roars

Melony Teague

The disciples went and woke him, saying, "Master, Master, we're going to drown!" He got up and rebuked the wind and the raging waters; the storm subsided, and all was calm. (Luke 8:24)

A low rumble of thunder woke me. It was followed by a flash of lightning and a much louder thunder's roar. I turned to my husband and said, "Wait for it." It was only moments before both of our kids were at our door asking if they could jump into our arms. My son then counted the seconds between lightning flashes and the thunder in order to gauge how far away the storm was.

Instinctively, my children knew where to go to feel safe. They knew that we would be waiting to welcome and enfold them. In no way would we ever consider saying to them, "Go away!" to deal with their insecurity alone.

When life's storms come your way, what is your instinctive response? Do you believe that your Father in heaven has arms open for you? Believing that God would in some way expect you to deal with your fears on your own is accepting a lie. Has God not already given the only begotten Son for you? Why would the Lord withhold comfort and refuge?

When the thunder roars in your life, when you feel that you are living through a storm, run to your heavenly Father. God is waiting to give you refuge. Even better, our Creator is able to still the storm.

PRAYER

Dear Jesus, please take my hand. Guide me to the safety of our Father's arms when storms overwhelm or frighten me. Thank you. Amen.

Let the Ink Flow

Remember a time when you faced a storm, either metaphorically or in reality. What emotions were in your heart? What part, if any, did your faith play in your experience?

PROMPT

Write about the storm experience and how your faith helped you through it.

Powerful Gift

Melony Teague

> The LORD smelled the pleasing aroma and said in his heart: "Never again will I curse the ground because of humans, even though every inclination of the human heart is evil from childhood. And never again will I destroy all living creatures, as I have done." (Genesis 8:21)

In Genesis 8:21 the word "inclination" can also be translated as "imagination." In the Scriptures we see two distinct sides to imagination: one here in Genesis 8:21, in which God calls our imaginings evil, and the other, in Ephesians 3:20, which indicates that even our most wonderful imaginings cannot measure up to the reality of what God can do.

It is rather humbling to think that our wildest, most fantastic, creative processes cannot measure up to the simplest truth of God's unfathomable being. When you consider writers like J. R. R. Tolkien and C. S. Lewis, whose imaginings have become legendary, do you think that God can do the same with yours? Why or why not?

Imagination is a powerful gift from God, one that is best given back to the Lord to guard. When it has been yielded to God, the Spirit can use your imagination to bring words of inspiration and encouragement to others.

"Now to him who is able to do immeasurably more than all we ask or imagine, according to his power that is at work within us, to him be glory in the church and in Christ Jesus throughout all generations, forever and ever! Amen" (Ephesians 3:20-21).

PRAYER

Dear Jesus, show me how to yield my imagination to you. Open my eyes to see as you see. Use my heart and mind for your glory. Amen.

Let the Ink Flow

Consider how God can use your imagination for glory. What obstacles stand in the way of you fully releasing your mind for use in expressing what God may show you?

PROMPT

Write about how you might overcome these challenges.

How Thirsty Are You?

Melony Teague

> Jesus answered, "Everyone who drinks this water will be thirsty again, but whoever drinks the water I give them will never thirst. Indeed, the water I give them will become in them a spring of water welling up to eternal life." The woman said to him, "Sir, give me this water so that I won't get thirsty and have to keep coming here to draw water." (John 4:13-15)

How thirsty are you? When your throat is parched, a large, cool glass of water seems sweet to the palate. When you are spiritually thirsty, do you attempt to satisfy your thirst with other things, like the woman at the well did, rather than drink from the water of life that we so desperately need? When was the last time your spiritual thirst was quenched?

Jesus says that those who seek will find, and that those who ask will receive (Matthew 7:7). But if we are not thirsty for the things of God, we are less likely to yearn for the satisfying living water that Jesus gives.

When we sit down to write, we draw from the inner well, which overflows onto the page. When we feel dry or feel as if we have nothing to give, Jesus is the one who will pour his living water, if we remember to ask.

PRAYER

Dear Jesus, I thank you that when I am thirsty for the spiritual things, you are there to offer living water. May I never grow so full that I feel less need of you. When I am dry, in need of your living water, remind me to ask. Amen.

Let the Ink Flow

REFLECTION

How does spending time with Jesus change your writing?

PROMPT

When you feel spiritually thirsty, how do you get to the source of the living water? Identify what you are thirsting for, what you long for, and write about your journey in finding the living water that you need in order to feel satisfied.

God's Time

Melony Teague

> There is a time for everything, and a season for every activity under the heavens. (Ecclesiastes 3:1)

Ecclesiastes 3:2-11 goes on to describe the various seasons in life, each one with its own timing.

When I looked out my window, I could see lingering snow on the ground and icicles hanging, even though the calendar declared the arrival of spring. Squirrels emerged from their hiding places, birds seemed to dance among the twigs of the leafless hedges. The sun reflected off the shimmering early morning snow. Every year without fail, my orange tulips and the purple crocuses had emerged in triumphant color and splendor. This time, I couldn't see the crocuses awaken and push through the grass as if to stretch and yawn after their annual sleep.

We go through frosty times in our lives when it is hard to believe that circumstances will get better. Seasons have been set in place since creation. There's something to be learned from the divine order of things.

The discomfort of staring at a blank page waiting for words to flow can be discouraging, but be reassured: it will not last forever. The season will end. The sun will shine to warm again. Hang on—spring flowers come just after the frost. April showers and summer storms are followed by a rainbow of promise. Words to be penned will come to mind once more.

Take heart. We know that our Creator is still at work, still making things new. Although our earthly senses beg to differ, our spiritual eyes can hold on to the truth—life is stirring, like a spring bulb, ready to burst forth in hope and joy when the time is right. God makes it all beautiful in time.

PRAYER

Dear Jesus, shine your light on me always as I turn my face to you. When I am discouraged, remind me of the seasons of life. Amen.

Let the Ink Flow

Do you ever question God's timing? Why and when?

In what way can you rest assured that God's timing is in your best interest? List a few of God's promises as a reminder to yourself when you are discouraged.

God of All Comfort

Melony Teague

Praise be to the God and Father of our Lord Jesus Christ, the Father
of compassion and the God of all comfort, who comforts us in all our
troubles, so that we can comfort those in any trouble with the comfort
we ourselves receive from God. For just as we share abundantly in the
sufferings of Christ, so also our comfort abounds through Christ. If we
are distressed, it is for your comfort and salvation; if we are comforted,
it is for your comfort, which produces in you patient endurance of the
same sufferings we suffer. And our hope for you is firm, because we
know that just as you share in our sufferings, so also you share in our
comfort. (2 Corinthians 1:3–7)

You sit down, intending to work on your latest writing project, and
your mind seems to be drawn back to the source of anguish deep
within. No matter how hard you try, you can't concentrate on the
task before you. Sound familiar?

Pain inflicted upon our souls, whether it be from a broken relationship or other excruciating circumstances, can be crippling to the
point where we are left feeling dazed and bruised.

It is comforting to know that Jesus himself suffered in emotional
ways. He wept over Jerusalem, was saddened by the loss of Lazarus,
and was touched with compassion for many whom he healed. His
suffering in the garden of Gethsemane was perhaps the most intense,
so much so that he prayed for hours while his disciples fell asleep.

Our comfort can come from the Father of compassion, the God
of all comfort; and through suffering we grow in patience and endurance. If we understand that these character traits are being formed
within us, our trials become easier to face. We confront them through
our hope in Christ, the one who suffered for us.

PRAYER

Dear Jesus, thank you that you suffered as I do. You did it for me,
my comforter. Help me to remember that I belong to the Father of
compassion, the God of all comfort. Amen.

Let the Ink Flow

When your anguish takes your focus away from your writing, consider praying and writing about how you feel and what you are going through. Once you have done that, you will be more likely to be able to get back to your work.

PROMPT

Write about an experience where writing has been part of the healing process for you.

Eat to Fill the Stomach

Melony Teague

> And he said to me, "Son of man, eat what is before you, eat this scroll; then go and speak to the people of Israel." So I opened my mouth, and he gave me the scroll to eat. Then he said to me, "Son of man, eat this scroll I am giving you and fill your stomach with it." So I ate it, and it tasted as sweet as honey in my mouth. He then said to me: "Son of man, go now to the people of Israel and speak my words to them. You are not being sent to a people of obscure speech and strange language, but to the people of Israel—not to many peoples of obscure speech and strange language, whose words you cannot understand. Surely if I had sent you to them, they would have listened to you." (Ezekiel 3:1-6)

The use of improper grammar today can cause us to feel like we have been sent to "a people of obscure speech and a strange language." The passage where God gives the word to Ezekiel to eat fascinates me. Is it possible that the words were penned and inspired by God to be sweet as honey and were given to "fill the stomach"?

Do you take time to eat and be filled by God's Word or other inspirational pieces? Is your focus on writing to feed others? It is interesting to note that Ezekiel had to open his mouth and eat in order to be filled, and that those words had a flavor.

Think about what words you eat daily. What flavor do they have? Are they sweet or bitter? Do they bring life or death? Are you hungry, or is your appetite for God's words satisfied daily? As you reflect on this, may your words be inspired, so that when you share them, they will bring the reader a sweet taste.

PRAYER

Dear Jesus, help me to remember that I need to feed my spirit with your Word. May I be filled and nourished so your words can linger in mine, bringing a taste of you to my readers. Amen.

Let the Ink Flow

As you reflect on today's devotion, refer back to the questions asked: How can you carve out more opportunities in your life to eat and be filled? When you examine your focus as a writer or speaker, what can you do to better feed others?

PROMPT

Write your responses in a poem, song, or other creative form.

Coming before God in Prayer

Claudia Loopstra

> The prayer of a righteous person is powerful and effective.
> (James 5:16b)

The Methodist minister and devotional writer E. M. Bounds (1835–1913) wrote nine of his eleven books on the subject of prayer. Obviously, he placed a great deal of importance on this topic. In reading a biography on Bounds, I learned that he took the directive of 1 Thessalonians 5:17, to "pray without ceasing," in a literal way. Prayer vigils were a part of his life, shaping what he had been led to write about. He believed that a person's heart is inclined to righteousness if consistency in praying is maintained on a day-to-day basis. If that is true, I think that the Holy Spirit will guide our talent as we prayerfully come before God, prior to sitting down at the keyboard.

The gift that God has given to us, through our ability to write, merits thoughtful prayer. Not only is it good to pray each day but also to pray before we take up the task of writing. As Christians, it is beneficial to ourselves and to God's kingdom here on earth to make every effort to give our best in being the conduit of God's purposes as we write.

Before your feet hit the floor in the morning, take some time for prayer—it may be short, but it will be effective when you belong to God through Jesus Christ.

PRAYER

Lord, help me to pray every day, before I start writing. Amen.

Let the Ink Flow

What reminder or prompt could you establish in order to start the habit of praying before you write? It could be a sticky-note, or a drawing, or some other visual. This will help you stay accountable to yourself and to God.

PROMPT

Do this for three weeks in a row. It will become a habit, one that will make a difference in your spiritual life and in your writing craft.

Where Does Your Inspiration Come From? (Part I)

Melony Teague

The LORD is good, a refuge in times of trouble. He cares for those who trust in him. (Nahum 1:7)

Often, the backstory of a well-known hymn can make the hymn even more poignant. "'Tis So Sweet to Trust in Jesus," by Louisa M. R. Stead, is one such hymn for me.

> 'Tis so sweet to trust in Jesus,
> and to take him at his word;
> just to rest upon his promise,
> and to know, "Thus saith the Lord."
> Jesus, Jesus, how I trust him!
> How I've proved him o'er and o'er!
> Jesus, Jesus, precious Jesus!
> O for grace to trust him more!

Louisa had suffered the shock of watching her husband die while attempting to save a drowning boy. Louisa was left poor, struggling to make ends meet and provide for her young daughter. Just when she needed it most, she found food and money left on her doorstep. It was then she penned this hymn that has encouraged many over the years. What a loss it would have been had she not written it!

Whether we are experiencing a joyful time, full of wonder and happiness, or whether we are heartbroken, life's lessons make us stronger and wiser and they shape our character. Trust Jesus more.

PRAYER

Dear Jesus, help me to trust you and remember that you focus not on my failure, but rather on my character being formed to be more like yours. Amen.

Let the Ink Flow

Take a moment to reflect on your challenges that have turned to praise.

Write a poem or a short reflection about a time when inspiration came out of hardship in your life.

Where Does Your Inspiration Come From? (Part II)

Melony Teague

Your eyes will see the king in his beauty and view a land that stretches afar. (Isaiah 33:17)

A blazing sunset or a riot of color within a field of blooms can inspire us to be creative and pen words that are beautiful to read. Love letters abound. Poetry as an ode to the beauty we see in others may fall to the page like the graceful snowfall in winter. Beauty and goodness are things that inspire; they get the creative juices flowing. They allow us to dream.

But what do you do when the skies are gray and there are no colorful blooms? When there is pain in your heart and your head is hung low, where do you get your inspiration? How, as the psalmist asks, can we sing God's songs in a strange land (Psalm 137:4)?

Some of the most beautiful words written have been born out of sorrow and pain. The Psalms are full of shining examples. As writers, we have the wonderful privilege, even when immersed in grief and agony, of digging out the beauty and the wonder of life as given by our God.

As a writer, if you face the pain and turn it to good use for others, your personal challenges may inspire and encourage others to overcome theirs.

PRAYER

Dear Jesus, help me to find the beauty hidden in my struggles and challenges and to share it with others. May my pain bring forth treasures for your glory as I choose to let life's trials build character in me. Thank you for always being there for me. May the sunshine and the rain be of equal inspiration to me, for it is you who shines within my heart. Amen.

Let the Ink Flow

Reflect on the beauty that you see around you and the inspiration that it brings. Perhaps there have been times when you have not been able to see beauty because of difficult circumstances. Think about how your inspiration or muse is affected in both scenarios.

PROMPT

Write a short story weaving together the thoughts and questions posed above to describe how you have been inspired to trust more or how bleak circumstances have affected your view of the world.

Where Does Your Inspiration Come From? (Part III)

Melony Teague

That each of them may eat and drink, and find satisfaction in all their toil—this is the gift of God. (Ecclesiastes 3:13)

In Parts I and II of "Where Does Your Inspiration Come From?" we explored finding inspiration in the beauty and wonder of things or in life's storms. What if inspiration also hides in the mundane? Can you uncover it? Some of my most meaningful inspiration has come when I have put on my earphones and vacuumed. Strange, but true—there is something about keeping the body busy while the mind works away. Listening to music helps me keep my brain occupied while my spirit stands ready to be inspired. As part of my side job, I vacuum for about four hours a week. Without fail, the same thing happens.

I think about the many written pieces, including some of the devotions in this book, that have come from my time while vacuuming. Would the same thing happen if I did not look for the extraordinary inspiration of the Holy Spirit in the mundane? I now count those hours of cleaning as a blessing. On the outside, it looks like I'm merely pushing a vacuum around. There is more going on than meets the eye.

Have you looked within the mundane for your inspiration? Chores can become times of thoughtful inspiration. One word of advice: have a small notepad tucked in your pocket or record voice memos on your phone. Capture your insights as they come to you. They are easily forgotten. You don't want to lose a great idea!

PRAYER

Dear Jesus, help me to use every opportunity, even if routine, to allow your inspiration to flow. Amen.

Let the Ink Flow

Which of the aspects discussed in the three-part devotion do you most relate to and why?

PROMPT

Write about where your inspiration comes from.

Showing Hospitality to Strangers

Glenda Dekkema

> Do not forget to show hospitality to strangers, for by so doing
> some people have shown hospitality to angels without knowing it.
> (Hebrews 13:2)

The first person to encourage me to become a writer was my seventh-grade teacher, who told me that I had the needed imagination, insight, and skills. This was a completely foreign idea to me because I didn't personally know any writers, so I dismissed the thought. Plus, my teacher didn't know how to dress properly—according to my "tween" brain—so what could he possibly know about anything? The second person was my high school English teacher, who said the same thing. And again, I crumpled up the thought and threw it in the trash, thinking that writing was only for highfalutin people who didn't need to pay bills or eat.

Dottie Walters, in her article "Angels over My Keyboard," tells us that when she was a teenager, her estranged father refused to pay for her college education. "Who cares?" he snarled to Dottie's mother. "She's not worth it."[1] This could have discouraged Dottie to the point of giving up. But it didn't.

Then she writes about her angel, Dr. Norman Vincent Peale. He encouraged her early on in her writing career: "I am so proud of you."[2] He later spoke to his publisher on her behalf to get her book *Never Underestimate the Selling Power of a Woman* published by Prentice Hall, which sold the entire first printing to Tupperware.

Angels are there to help us at times when we least expect it. They are all around us. They are there to spontaneously encourage us when help isn't sought—as in my case—and sometimes we need to be brave enough to ask someone to support and encourage us.

PRAYER

Lord, send your angels to encourage my writing, and help me recognize when I am in their presence. Thank you, Lord. Amen.

Let the Ink Flow

When have you experienced angels of encouragement in your life? Say a prayer to thank God for these individuals.

If you haven't experienced any angels in your life, ask someone to help or encourage you. Write about how it made you feel to ask for help. Describe how the help felt "angelic."

1. Dottie Walters, "Angels over My Keyboard," in *Chicken Soup for the Writer's Soul: Stories to Open the Heart and Rekindle the Spirit of Writers*, ed. Jack Canfield, Mark Victor Hansen, and Bud Gardner (Deerfield Beach, FL: Health Communications, 2000), 186.

2. Ibid., 189.

Know Yourself

Tech-Detox

Carol Ford

"I have the right to do anything," you say—but not everything is beneficial.
"I have the right to do anything"—but I will not be mastered by anything.
(1 Corinthians 6:12)

The term "tech-detox" is being used extensively in articles and books. Dr. Gregory Jantz, in his book *#Hooked: The Pitfalls of Media, Technology and Social Networking*, describes it as follows: "There are times you need to log off, power down, disconnect, and untether yourself from all this stuff; it's been called a 'tech-detox,' for lack of a better term."[1]

I have to admit that I am finding it hard to use the "off switch" to texting, emails, blogging, and so on. I love the ability to connect this way. Social media suits my extroverted personality. I'm noticing that it also offers a conduit for individuals who tend toward introversion; they can express themselves without the need for face-to-face communication.

Similar to Paul's warning in today's Scripture concerning "profitable" things, Dr. Jantz writes, "The ultimate filter for whether something is good or bad for us isn't how we feel about it or how much fun it is or even how efficient it makes us. The ultimate filter for every part of our lives is God. God is not ignorant of technology; it is his world and his creation that make it possible."[2]

Technology is not going away. Writers who want to be published, network, and source information must be connected. Technology is not the enemy, but we must learn to use it wisely instead of being "mastered" by it. Let's call on our Creator to help us to exercise self-control over our own creation.

PRAYER

Dear Lord, thank you for technology. Give me your wisdom and guidance as I use it to honor you. Amen.

Let the Ink Flow

How do you spend your time? How much time have you spent on the computer and technology during the last week? Prayerfully consider how you can make your writing, devotional life, and Christian service a priority.

PROMPT

Write a journal entry about today's topic and how it impacts your writing.

NOTES

1. Gregory L. Jantz, with Ann McMurray, *#Hooked: The Pitfalls of Media, Technology and Social Networking* (Lake Mary, FL: Siloam, 2012), 10.
2. Ibid.

Cleaning the Cupboard

Carol Ford

> For no one can lay any foundation other than the one already laid, which is Jesus Christ. If anyone builds on this foundation using gold, silver, costly stones, wood, hay or straw, their work will be shown for what it is, because the Day will bring it to light. It will be revealed with fire, and the fire will test the quality of each person's work. (1 Corinthians 3:11-13)

Products stale, expired, and of no interest to my taste buds spilled out of my kitchen cupboard. I pushed on the contents so I could shut the door. Rice cakes, 100-calorie snacks, vanilla protein mix—you get the picture.

This cupboard was an eyesore, and buying these items was a mistake; I needed to let them go. Once I accepted the fact that keeping this food was not going to change anything, only then could I find the resolve to throw them out.

In an accounting class a few years ago I learned the term "sunk costs." This concept has always stayed with me. A "sunk cost" is money already spent that cannot be retrieved, and throwing more money or time into that investment is not going to improve the situation or recover the losses.

As writers, we can find it hard to distance ourselves from situations, projects, and other things that are cluttering up our life and mind. We say to ourselves, "I need to do this or that, and then I will start writing." Or, "I've put too many hours into this piece to scrap it now."

Moving on is difficult, but when we resign ourselves to this decision, there is a great sense of release and freedom.

PRAYER

Dear Jesus, help me to know how to let go of clutter that is robbing me of my best efforts and work. Amen.

Let the Ink Flow

In light of today's Scripture, what "cupboards" do you need to clean today? This may be related to your writing, or maybe it is something else that is cluttering up your life.

PROMPT

How can you implement what you have learned in this devotion? Write down some ideas.

Sluggard

Glenda Dekkema

I went past the field of the sluggard, past the vineyard of someone who has no sense; thorns had come up everywhere, the ground was covered with weeds, and the stone wall was in ruins. I applied my heart to what I observed and learned a lesson from what I saw: A little sleep, a little slumber, a little folding of the hands to rest—and poverty will come on you like a thief and scarcity like an armed man. (Proverbs 24:30-34)

There is a big difference between being slothful and taking appropriate and much-needed rest. I know when I'm being slothful and when I'm in the company of other sloths, and we're happily picking fleas off each other. Other times it is less clear.

We writers usually work in isolation, with no supervisor other than God to judge if we are managing laziness versus productive writing time, adequate rest, and our obligations.

But there are less obvious means of laziness. I prefer writing to doing the household chores. To refuse to do these menial tasks so that I can write the "Great Canadian Novel" while my family scavenges for food and clean clothes is slothful.

Perhaps slothfulness is found where we don't expect it, such as spending too much time multitasking or social networking, where nothing really gets done well; in self-criticism or gossip; in neglecting to exercise; or in anxiety because we don't lift our fears to God.

On the other hand—and this is also a judgment call requiring wisdom—perhaps we need to set aside some of our other duties so that we can meet our writing deadlines. This proverb talks about the sluggard as someone who has no sense. Let's be sensible and balanced in all we do.

PRAYER

Dear Lord, help me to distinguish among being slothful, being in the creative flow, and caring for others and myself as you command. Help me to distinguish between being ambitious and overly ambitious. Amen.

Let the Ink Flow

Plan to divide your workday into productive writing time, caring for self—including adequate rest—and fulfilling other duties. It's better to be realistic than overly ambitious so that you will be able to maintain this working arrangement.

PROMPT

How much time do you intend to devote to each category? Draw up a schedule to help keep you on track.

Time Challenge

Marguerite Cummings

If there were two of me
And so much less to do
I might get this to thee
In just an hour or two . . .

But time is short
And I must run
Catch up with chores
Still be a mom!

What shall I say?
What shall I do?
Can't stop to think!
                    Run to the Son

A scream
A sigh
A cry
—That's all

He knows
He cares
He'll guide
                    Move on

PRAYER

Dear Jesus, please calm me and show me your way. Amen.

Let the Ink Flow

How do you think God wants you to spend your time?

What might you have to give up in order to accomplish this? Write about it.

A Light on My Path

Glenda Dekkema

Your word is a lamp for my feet, a light on my path. (Psalm 119:105)

I am a member of what is commonly called the "sandwich generation," people who feel obligated to attend to the needs of older family members as well as younger ones. But in terms of sandwiches,
I often feel more like I am muddling along with the "sloppy joe"
crowd—letting life's messiness distract me and cause me to wander
from the path that God sets before me. It's all too easy to lose sight
of what are priorities and what are trivialities.

But no matter how busy I get, I never completely abandon my
writing career. God keeps leading me back to my desk and computer
because it is what God wants me to do. Is this how you feel?

I will not allow busyness and scatteredness to darken and obscure
God's path. Will you? It's very easy to become blinded by the chaos
and mess around us. But, if we pay attention and look, we will see
the light of God's Word showing the way.

PRAYER

Lord, despite any busyness, may I always take the time for you and
your purpose. Thank you for lighting my path. Amen.

Let the Ink Flow

Despite your busy schedule, are you able to take enough time to write? Why or why not? How do you manage to fit it all in?

PROMPT

Write about how, despite the many snares of our modern lifestyle, you plan to remain solidly on God's path.

Chipping Away

Marguerite Cummings

Chipping, chipping, chipping away
I'll be chipping away at my workload today

> Feels like a huge block of ice, as high as can be
> Much too hard to break up, far too much for me
> *I can't do it, just can't do it*

Yet I'll be chipping, chipping, chipping away
I'll be chipping away at my workload today

> Just do a little corner, and that's enough
> The Son will help you, and it won't be so rough
> *Do it early, do it early*

Yes, just get chipping, chipping, chipping away
Just get chipping away at your workload today

> You must use the right tools, they'll need to be sharp
> Ice is tough to break up, you'll need to be smart
> *And be patient, and be patient*

So keep chipping, chipping, chipping away
Just keep chipping away at your workload today

> Think of the spring, when the ice will be gone
> The Son will shine brightly, your job will be DONE
> *Thank you Jesus, thank you Jesus*

Meanwhile keep chipping, chipping, chipping away
Just keep on chipping away at your workload today
Yes, keep chipping, chipping, chipping away
Yes, I'll keep chipping away at my workload today

> *Thank you Jesus, thank you Jesus*

Let the Ink Flow

Think of another picture for "chipping away" during the long summer months—such as the ants in the Bible that work ceaselessly (Proverbs 30:25).

PROMPT

Become a songwriter for a day and compose some lyrics about your thoughts on this.

The Next Generation

Carol Ford

I will utter . . . things we have heard and known, things our ancestors
have told us. We will not hide them from their descendants; we will tell
the next generation the praiseworthy deeds of the LORD, his power,
and the wonders he has done. (Psalm 78:2b-4)

I was adopted into a Christian family when I was five years old. At
the age of fifty, I searched and found my birth family. Shortly into my
new relationship with the family, I received the most beautiful letter
from my birth mother's sister. I quote here what my Aunt Lois wrote:

"I praise and thank the Lord for his care over you. I just can't
get over feeling from the day I first saw you, you were part of me
and even before. Once you were lost (to us) but now you are found.
What a precious gem. I often think of Grandma Beatty—she would
pray that all my Mom's children would come to know the Lord—
even though she didn't name each one specifically. God knew, and
has honored faithful prayers in many ways. I love you—we are lively
stones bonded together by the Holy Spirit. Love, Auntie."

My aunt has now passed away. Her letter remains; it reveals this
wonderful knowledge of the prayers of my great grandmother. The
writing also tells of "yes" answers to earlier prayers, answers that the
person praying was no longer alive to see.

I am currently writing my memoir. It is my story as an adopted
child who yearned to know her past, her midlife search for her birth
family, and the awareness of God's protection throughout her life.

As writers, we have a special gift and opportunity to pass on stories and encouragement to future generations. You may never know
what impact your prayers and writing will have on the lives of individuals for years to come.

PRAYER

Dear Lord, thank you for your wisdom and guidance in my writing
today; help me to create compelling and inspirational content and
communicate God's love to future generations. Amen.

Let the Ink Flow

What spiritual legacy would you like to leave?

Write a short story of an event in your life, a time when you experienced God's protection, guidance, or blessing. How could you share this with your family either verbally or in writing?

Life Stories

Carol Ford

> On one of these journeys I was going to Damascus with the authority and commission of the chief priests. About noon, King Agrippa, as I was on the road, I saw a light from heaven, brighter than the sun, blazing around me and my companions. We all fell to the ground, and I heard a voice saying to me in Aramaic, "Saul, Saul, why do you persecute me? It is hard for you to kick against the goads." (Acts 26:12-14)

Memoirs are not biographies or autobiographies that document our whole life. Instead, they focus on life experiences that will engage and excite the reader. They provide context without day-to-day or year-to-year detail.

In Acts 26, Scripture offers an excellent example of how we can provide context for our life stories.

Paul briefly shared his past and then focused on his most profound life-changing experience: his encounter with Christ on the road to Damascus. He includes dialogue to recreate his dramatic conversion.

In a true short story about my adoptive mother, I chose to write about only what happened three days prior to her death. I focused on this incident because it had a profound effect on me. I was at her bedside with a visiting pastor when she spoke these words: "This is my beautiful daughter, Carol. She has been a wonderful daughter to me and I love her so much." These were expressions of love that she had never shared with me before, and it would be several years before I understood that in those final hours she had given me her "blessing." I entitled the story "My Mother's Gift," and it was accepted for publication.

When we feature the most impactful life events in our writing, it is then that we touch the hearts of our readers.

PRAYER

Lord, help me today to write about events and life-changing experiences in ways that will make my life story interesting and focused on you. Amen.

Let the Ink Flow

Think about your fondest memory, picture, or scene and recall how you felt.

Write a short piece that captures one of your life events—for example, meeting your spouse, a trip to an exciting destination, an illness, or the day you became a Christian.

Our God Stories

Glenda Dekkema

> As Jesus was getting into the boat, the man who had been demon-possessed begged to go with him. Jesus did not let him, but said, "Go home to your own people and tell them how much the Lord has done for you, and how he has had mercy on you." (Mark 5:18-19)

Most, if not all, Christian writers have a story about redemption and the power of God. These may be their most powerful narratives. Many people are drawn to writing careers because they feel compelled to tell what is heaviest on their hearts.

There are many stories in the Bible about healing and redemption. In Mark 5:18-19, Jesus healed a man, possessed by evil spirits, who had led an isolated, miserable life. The grateful man went to the city to tell everyone about what Jesus had done for him. Everyone was amazed at this transformation.

Hot Apple Cider and *A Second Cup of Hot Apple Cider* are anthologies of writings by Canadian Christians who have overcome obstacles through the grace of God. Some of the stories are fiction, but they are just as powerful as the nonfiction ones because they discuss a certain truth about God's redemptive love. Jesus tells us to share our stories with anyone who will listen. Writing them down and having them published is a great way to reach a wider audience than friends and family.

My first published story, "I Became a Mother on Mother's Day,"[1] is my God story. It describes how my husband and I struggled with infertility—the anxiety, the physical, emotional, social, and spiritual pain, and finally the miraculous adoption of our first child. I hope that our God stories are able to reach others struggling with similar issues.

PRAYER

Dear Lord, if it honors you, help me to tell my story for your glory. Amen.

Let the Ink Flow

What is your God story? Have you written it yet? If not, what is holding you back?

Would you like to write your God story now? You may wish to share it with someone or submit it for publication somewhere.

1. Glenda Dekkema de Vries, "I Became a Mother on Mother's Day," *The Globe and Mail*, May 8, 2009 (http://www.theglobeandmail.com/life/parenting/mothers-day/i-became-a-mother-on-mothers-day/article4318447/).

Truth—Stranger than Fiction

Melony Teague

> When Elisha reached the house, there was the boy lying dead on his couch. He went in, shut the door on the two of them and prayed to the LORD. Then he got on the bed and lay on the boy, mouth to mouth, eyes to eyes, hands to hands. As he stretched himself out on him, the boy's body grew warm. Elisha turned away and walked back and forth in the room and then got on the bed and stretched out on him once more. The boy sneezed seven times and opened his eyes. (2 Kings 4:32-35)

After the boy's mother begged Elisha to take action, an unusual series of events played out. When we read passages like this one, it sometimes seems to us that truth is stranger than fiction. Perhaps, though, since we are reading the story with our limited human understanding, we can't seem to make sense of why Elisha did what he did. What may seem even stranger are the boy's seven sneezes. Why sneezes? Why seven? Varied interpretations are possible, but the bottom line is that the boy was revived.

Our own story may seem just as strange. Sometimes our faith is tested. I find this Scripture verse comforting: "For now we see only a reflection as in a mirror; then we shall see face to face. Now I know in part; then I shall know fully, even as I am fully known" (1 Corinthians 13:12).

Know that one day, when you get to the end of your life's earthly book, you will finally know all things as you step into the presence of the all-knowing God. Isn't that an exciting thought? Meanwhile, let's tell our own strange-but-true stories of a life of faith in Christ.

PRAYER

Dear Jesus, when I read Bible stories like this one, I realize how limited my understanding is. Help me, when my faith is tested, to be obedient to whatever you ask of me. Amen.

Let the Ink Flow

Take some time to reflect on the devotion for today. What was your reaction when you read the strange-but-true story?

PROMPT

Have you had an experience in which you felt that you had to do something strange in order to be obedient to God? If so, write about it. If not, write about something strange that you thought God might have been prompting you to do, and later you regretted that you hadn't done it.

Well-Being

In the Dark

Carol Ford

"Therefore I tell you, do not worry about your life, what you will eat or drink; or about your body, what you will wear. Is not life more than food, and the body more than clothes? Look at the birds of the air; they do not sow or reap or store away in barns, and yet your heavenly Father feeds them. Are you not much more valuable than they? Can any one of you by worrying add a single hour to your life?" (Matthew 6:25-27)

Our thoughts and concerns during the night seem magnified. We are often steeped in doubts and fears. Do you ever wake up early in the morning already thinking about your commitments and worries? Does your stomach go into knots as you feel overwhelmed? You are not alone. Many of us share this same experience. The following prayer formed in my mind during one of these early morning episodes. I wrote it down to share with you. May this peace, God's peace, calm your soul and inspire creative writing today.

PRAYER

Thoughts
Lord, come into my thoughts
Fill my mind with love
Take away my bitter spirit
Give me grace from above

Lord, come into my thoughts
Fill my mind with hope
Take away my fears and doubts
Give me strength to cope

Lord, come into my thoughts
Fill my mind with praise
Take away my worldly cares
Give me peace today
Amen.

Let the Ink Flow

Commit Matthew 6:25-27 to memory, and bring it to mind in times of restlessness, fearfulness, and anxiousness.

PROMPT

Write a letter to God today expressing your love and gratitude for his abiding love and care, especially during dark times.

Moving Mountains

Glenda Dekkema

"Truly I tell you, if you have faith as small as a mustard seed, you can say to this mountain, 'Move from here to there,' and it will move. Nothing will be impossible for you." (Matthew 17:20b)

Many writers struggle with addiction. Some say that they need a drink to relax, and others that they need drugs to tap into the recesses of their minds. Someone asked Stephen King, "Do you drink?" to which he replied, "Of course, I just said I was a writer."[1]

I recently watched the movie *Limitless*. Bradley Cooper's character takes an illegal street drug that gives him superhuman strength, physical ability, wisdom, and intelligence. He doesn't behave like the average junkie; instead, he acts like a perfectly normal human being, except that he can move mountains if he wants to. He becomes addicted to his newly found godlike abilities, and he continues to take the pills to the point of self-destruction.

God says that we can move mountains with our faith alone. We don't need drugs or alcohol—not even Belgian chocolates—to raise us to new heights. We just need to trust God, for nothing is impossible with him. Wow! I would like to stretch that to "We can move mountains with our faithful writing."

PRAYER

Gracious God, thank you for reminding me that nothing is impossible for you. Amen.

Let the Ink Flow

Think about mountains in your life that need to be moved. Where do you get your strength to move them?

PROMPT

Write about your biggest mountain—what it is and how you plan to overcome it.

NOTES

1. https://www.goodreads.com/quotes/search?commit=Search&page=5& q=stephen+king&utf8=%E2%9C%93.

The View from the Couch

Carol Ford

> "Come to me, all you who are weary and burdened, and I will give you rest. Take my yoke upon you and learn from me, for I am gentle and humble in heart, and you will find rest for your souls. For my yoke is easy and my burden is light." (Matthew 11:28-30)

I recently spent several weeks lying flat on my back. This was the first time I'd experienced anything like this, and my life was on hold; I had to cancel all my commitments. In some ways it gave me a feeling of freedom. No one expected anything of me; I had to let go and give up control.

This pause in my busy life provided time for reflection and meditation. It was a time of renewal in my faith—time for prayer and reading God's Word.

My friends' visits, as a result of my being housebound, provided unexpected joy. My well-wishers seemed to adopt the same peaceful rest that I was experiencing. We talked and shared with no hurry or need to rush, much differently than we would at a coffee shop or over lunch. Our conversations seemed more intimate and transparent. I felt blessed to have good friends.

There may be something that has stopped you from writing—a death, a sick family member, or some other personal crisis. You may feel discouraged and wonder why this is happening or how it fits into God's will for your life.

When something stops us from our writing—perhaps a death, a sick family member, or a personal illness, feelings of discouragement and questions about how this fits into God's will for our lives can flood our minds. In these situations we need to lean on Christ and rise above the clouds into the sunshine.

PRAYER

Lord, thank you for the ability to praise you despite my circumstances. Help me to use this trial to add insight into my writing. Amen.

Let the Ink Flow

In these two columns, list your struggles on one side, and on the other side list a positive response. Prayerfully reframing your difficulties can give you a new perspective.

Struggle	Positive Response
example: I'm in much pain.	example: I'm thankful for pain medication.

PROMPT

Now write a short piece on the blessings that you can see in your struggles.

I Just Dropped a Jam Jar

Marguerite Cummings

I just dropped a jam jar
My life is in a mess
I just dropped a jam jar
I think this is a test

     Of patience and of stamina
     Just like the past nine weeks
     Of doctors, tests, and hospitals
     Emotions and no sleep

Tomorrow is key surgery
A lot is on my mind
I wonder what the tests will bring
We all just feel so blind

     And now glass shards are everywhere
     And tears come flowing down
     My floor is a disaster zone
     Just like my life right now

But then I catch a paper
To wrap the sticky mess
It talks of children starving
Of millions close to death

     My heart turns to our privilege
     To have so much so fast
     To see doctors tomorrow
     When others get bypassed

I have to say a prayer
Of thanks, wonder, and praise
Of pain and of compassion
Will I still be the same?

     And now my kitchen floor is clean
     The time I spent in prayer
     Has truly put my mind at peace
     Praise God for
          Being there

Let the Ink Flow

Reflect on Psalm 105:4: "Look to the LORD and his strength; seek his face always."

PROMPT

This poem is a gentle reminder that even when things get very tough, there is no need to give in to self-pity. How do you deal with situations that seem out of control, unfair, or overwhelming? Try writing a poem about this.

That's a Good Deal

Glenda Dekkema

Take delight in the LORD, and he will give you the desires of your heart.
(Psalm 37:4)

Recently, in one of my spiritual "Aha!" moments, I read this Scripture verse and thought, "That's a good deal!" It's so easy to delight in the Lord. And the reward is so great! God will give me the desires of my heart? Really?

I wondered how I could squeeze every ounce of goodness out of this promise. I was quite excited. First, I would have to truly delight in the Lord, which has elements of rapture and surprise. Second, I would have to know what the desires of my heart are so that I can tell God.

To complicate matters a little, my desires would have to be in keeping with the Lord's will, and I don't necessarily know what that is. I had the good sense to know that if the desire of my heart was for a brand-new, thirty-two-foot sailboat, I probably wouldn't get it. But, if my desire was for my writing career to benefit others in some way, my request would be answered.

I went for walks with God and opened up my eyes to the wonders of his ways. Yes, I could gaze up at the stars and marvel at the complexity of the galaxies, but that type of rapture was missing the element of surprise.

It is now my habit to look, feel, listen, and even smell the hidden wonders of his magnificence. Today I saw bright yellow mushrooms with red polka dots high up in a tree, off the beaten path, for no one to see except someone like me who is on a "delight in the Lord" mission.

PRAYER

Dear Lord, help me to spend some time every day to delight in you and your magnificence. Amen.

Let the Ink Flow

Go on a "delight in the Lord" mission. Open up all your senses.

PROMPT

Write a detailed description of one of the things you delighted in today. You may want to keep a journal and do it every day.

Turning Tragedy into Music (Part 1)

Glenda Dekkema

He put a new song in my mouth, a hymn of praise to our God. Many will see and fear the LORD and put their trust in him. (Psalm 40:3)

While my uncle, Peter Dekkema, has struggled with cancer for decades, his faith has remained strong. In his quest to inspire and motivate others in their faith, he teamed up with Don Reeves to write lyrics for their four albums.

I asked my uncle if I could use some of his lyrics for the devotional that my friends and I were working on. He looked at me in silence for a while, and then his eyes welled up with tears. He said, "A while ago I dreamt I was standing at the gates of heaven, wanting to enter. Jesus said, 'I'm not finished with you yet. Go back down.'" After he woke up, he wrote the lyrics to this song, "Go Back Down."[1]

> I had a dream
> God had called me home
> And the gates of heaven opened wide
> But I could not step inside
> I wanted so much to stay
> But I was told, I'd have to go
> And I was sent back down
> I had to help God's kingdom grow
> (*Refrain*)
> I had to go back down
> My time on earth was not done
> Tell everybody about God's Son

PRAYER

Lord, remind us that, regardless of our health or situation, as long as we live and breathe, our time on earth is not yet done. Help us to remain faithful in what we believe, say, do, and write. Amen.

Let the Ink Flow

Do you feel that God isn't finished with you yet? Why or why not?

PROMPT

Write about what you think that God still wants you to do.

NOTES

1. Peter Dekkema and Don Reeves, "Go Back Down," *Broken Man.* Used by permission.

Turning Tragedy into Music (Part II)

Glenda Dekkema

> Remember your Creator in the days of your youth, before the days of trouble come and the years approach when you will say, "I find no pleasure in them." (Ecclesiastes 12:1)

My grandfather (Peter's dad) suffered with Alzheimer's for the final years of his life. In the earlier phase of the disease, to the astonishment of his family, he was still able to recite the Lord's Prayer. Unfortunately, over time he forgot who everyone was, including his own wife, children, and grandchildren. But I know that God never forgot *him*.

> *"Remember Me"*[1]
> (*Refrain*)
> Oh Lord, I remember you
> And I believe
> Though I don't remember myself
> I may forget who I am in the autumn of my days
> As my memories like the autumn leaves all fall away
> The colors that I knew aren't there anymore
> If my mind should go
> And I should forget all my paths
> Oh Lord, oh Lord, please remember me

PRAYER

Dear Lord, in all that I do, in my writing, conversations, day-to-day routine, relationships, hobbies, and duties, from this day, through old age and forevermore, may I remember you. Amen.

Let the Ink Flow

You are on God's mind. Think about some ways God has shown this to you.

Write a poem about your desire to remember God throughout your life. Consider composing a simple melody and turn your poem into music.

NOTES

1. Peter Dekkema and Don Reeves, "Remember Me," *Fire in My Heart.* Used by permission.

May Your Will Be Done

Glenda Dekkema

> Then Jesus went with his disciples to a place called Gethsemane,
> and he said to them, "Sit here while I go over there and pray." He took
> Peter and the two sons of Zebedee along with him, and he began to be
> sorrowful and troubled. . . . Going a little farther, he fell with his face to
> the ground and prayed, "My Father, if it is possible, may this cup be taken
> from me. Yet not as I will, but as you will." (Matthew 26:36-37,39)

A famous study on depression by Dr. Nancy Andreasen at Iowa's
Writers' Workshop found that 80 percent of writers surveyed met
the diagnostic criteria for clinical depression (also known as major
depressive disorder) at one time or another.[1]

We don't know if depressed people are attracted to writing, or if
the nature of the job—including isolation, potential rejection, and
low pay—is the culprit.

Christians are not immune to depression, despite our faith. It is
comforting to know that Jesus himself, even though sinless, was capable of being "sorrowful and troubled." What's more, Jesus offers
a perfect example of how to deal with hardship, more hardship than
any of us will ever face. Consider the theme of his prayer at Gethsemane and in the prayer that he taught his disciples: "May your will
be done." Jesus, even in his darkest moments, expressed trust and
faith in God's presence and plan.

PRAYER

Lord, be with me when I become disillusioned, sad, or depressed.
Allow me not to feel ashamed, and help me to seek professional assistance when needed. May your will be done. Amen.

Let the Ink Flow

Consider a time in your life—or it may be right now—in which you or someone you know experienced depression, and describe the experience.

PROMPT

Write creatively about that experience of depression, whether it was yours or someone else's.

NOTES

1. For a precise description of clinical depression, see *Diagnostic and Statistical Manual of Mental Disorders: DSM-5* (Washington, DC: American Psychiatric Publishing, 2013).

The Insomniac

Glenda Dekkema

For [the LORD] grants sleep to those he loves. (Psalm 127:2b)

Writers feel intensely, think deeply, see vividly, and hear acutely, which perhaps makes us the most anxious, hollow-eyed, and sleep-deprived people on the planet. And so Bible passages about rest are important for us. God understands. It's as if the Lord is offering us freshly laundered, sun-dried sheets, smoothed over a pillow-top mattress.

I asked a pastor friend of mine, who assures me that he can drink two cups of coffee after dinner and still fall soundly asleep, how he manages to defeat insomnia despite all that caffeine. In addition, I asked how he is able to sleep so soundly when he has to deal with so many urgent, possibly grave and intense, church matters. He told me that every night he prays, "Lord, I can't handle these issues, but you can. I commit these problems to you."

PRAYER

Lord, there are so many things over which I have little or no control. Please help me to find my rest in you. Lord, I can't handle these issues, but you can. I commit these problems to you. Amen.

Let the Ink Flow

How well are you sleeping? Do you pray before falling asleep? Why or why not?

Write about a particular night in which you were unable to sleep. What was going on in your life and mind that kept you up?

Strength

Glenda Dekkema

> He gives strength to the weary and increases the power of the weak. Even youths grow tired and weary, and young men stumble and fall; but those who hope in the LORD will renew their strength. They will soar on wings like eagles; they will run and not grow weary, they will walk and not be faint. (Isaiah 40:29-31)

About a week prior to my dad's scheduled surgery, my mother prayed to God asking for strength for herself to endure as his caregiver. On the day of his operation she had a mini-stroke. You and I might think that this was a strange answer to her prayer!

My mother was the main support person for my dad, who battled cancer for more than a decade and recently passed away from the disease. She nursed him, drove him to all his appointments, managed his complicated medical intervention, and provided daily emotional and physical support. Their retirement plans were constantly being interrupted by his illness. At the time, she asked herself, "When will this end? When can we enjoy life again?"

When she was in the hospital recovering from her stroke, she considered God's answer to her request for strength. After some thought, she concluded that this was God's will, although she didn't fully understand the reasons.

As writers and as human beings, we may grow weary. We may pray for recognition for our writing efforts—surely this will restore our strength. God may have something else in mind. We may not know what it is, and we may not like the answer, but we can trust that it is all a part of God's plan.

PRAYER

Lord, sometimes I feel tired. Sometimes I need my strength restored. The ways in which you answer my request for strength may be different from what I expect. My trust is in you. Amen.

Let the Ink Flow

Open your eyes. Look around for ways that God is working to build you up.

Have you ever had a time in your life in which your prayers were answered differently than you had hoped? Tell your story about how God is working in your life.

Never Alone

Melony Teague

> The LORD God said, "It is not good for the man to be alone. I will make a helper suitable for him." (Genesis 2:18)

Repeatedly, this pattern emerges: it's God's plan that we have companionship, whether from a spouse, a friend, or a fellow believer. God does not want anyone to be alone. In fact, Scripture reminds us, "God sets the lonely in families, he leads out the prisoners with singing; but the rebellious live in a sun-scorched land" (Psalm 68:6).

Many times when we feel alone, the first instinct is to look for comfort. At the school where I work, children come to me. I often hear, "So-and-so doesn't want to be my friend." They feel alone and excluded. My advice to them, as I wipe away their little tears, is this: "Look around the play area. Find someone who is alone. Be a friend to that person."

We can find comfort in knowing that these seemingly insignificant playground spats do not go unnoticed, for if God is concerned about a sparrow, how much more God will concern himself with kindergarten insecurities. "Are not two sparrows sold for a penny? Yet not one of them will fall to the ground outside your Father's care" (Matthew 10:29).

When you are feeling most alone, to whom do you turn? Do you have a writing companion who is there for you? Sometimes we isolate ourselves, since nowadays we are expected to be independent rather than interdependent. It is almost assumed that we'll get on with things on our own, we'll cope on our own and that is that. But there is no weakness in seeking company. In fact, Genesis suggests that we are made for companionship. Best of all, God seeks out *our* company each day. Let's remember to welcome the Spirit.

PRAYER

Dear Jesus, when I feel alone, help me to look around, to reach out to the persons you have chosen for me. Thank you that you are always there for me. Amen.

Let the Ink Flow

How does this topic make you feel? Does it strike a chord within your heart? Is it something you would rather not discuss? If you have been hurt when you've reached out in the past, ask God to help you forgive and heal from the experience.

PROMPT

Once you have prayed, write your reflections here.

Personalities

The Nature of a Writer

Melony Teague

> Shout for joy, you heavens; rejoice, you earth; burst into song, you mountains! For the LORD comforts his people and will have compassion on his afflicted ones. (Isaiah 49:13)

Do you get the picture? Fortunately for us, God is slow to anger. Read Psalm 145:8 and Matthew 9:36.

We are asked to do the same for one another as brothers and sisters of God's kingdom. We need to reach out to those who do not know this compassionate God, and we have been given clear instruction on how to do it too: "Be kind and compassionate to one another, forgiving each other, just as in Christ God forgave you" (Ephesians 4:32). As God's people, we are to put on spiritual clothes as described in this verse: "Therefore, as God's chosen people, holy and dearly loved, clothe yourselves with compassion, kindness, humility, gentleness and patience" (Colossians 3:12).

This concept is not hard for us to grasp, until it clashes with the competitive or ambitious side of our writer's nature. In the writer's world, we may be called on to be fighters or pioneers. When we are determined, we may be labeled "go-getters," relentless in our pursuit to get that article published, that book written, or some similar goal. We can be our own worst critics.

Nothing kills the creative process faster than exhaustion. Take a step back. Have you been pushing too hard? When you don't meet your self-imposed standards, how do you react? Treating ourselves with compassion seems to go against the writer's grain at times, but how about giving it a try?

PRAYER

Dear Jesus, you are the ultimate example of how we are to be compassionate to others. You extended compassion to me. Help me to grasp the idea that I also need to be compassionate toward myself at times and to realize when I am in need of it. Amen.

Let the Ink Flow

Why do you think we are our own worst critic? Think about ways in which you can extend compassion toward yourself.

Write down the effects of self-criticism on your life and work. How does it affect you emotionally and mentally? Write about the benefits of being kind to yourself. What are your thoughts on developing a healthy attitude of compassion toward yourself?

Parts of the Body

Glenda Dekkema

> But in fact God has placed the parts in the body, every one of them, just as he wanted them to be. If they were all one part, where would the body be? As it is, there are many parts but one body. The eye cannot say to the hand, "I don't need you!" And the head cannot say to the feet, "I don't need you!" On the contrary, those parts of the body that seem to be weaker are indispensable, and the parts that we think are less honorable we treat with special honor. (1 Corinthians 12:18-22)

Have you ever felt that your part is trivial in God's master plan? Have you ever doubted your purpose? Or wondered if you even had one? Are you jealous of more successful writers?

Do you write fiction or nonfiction? Are you a poet, blogger, editor? Or a copywriter, preacher, Sunday school teacher? Or, have you ever tried being a ghost writer or a cartoonist?

All of us have a role, and we are, according to Scripture, equally important in the eyes of the Lord. We shouldn't doubt the gifts that we have been given by our faithful and omnipotent God. He is the one who made us, and he is the one who loves and appreciates us for who we are, and for what we are capable of.

Listen again to what the Scripture is telling us: "those parts of the body that seem to be weaker are indispensable." Whenever I feel inadequate or untalented or incapable of producing anything meaningful, I think about this passage. At whatever stage I am at in my writing career, God is blessing it because God sees what I am doing as something important.

PRAYER

Dear Lord, I have a part to play in the body of believers. May I feel confident enough to fulfill the duties you have laid out for me, using the unique talents you have given me. Amen.

Let the Ink Flow

Prayerfully consider: To what body part would you compare yourself? Why?

PROMPT

Describe yourself as a writer—your strengths and your weaknesses. Write about how that identity and these gifts might "fit" into Christ's body.

Perfectionism

Carol Ford

> Not that I have already obtained all this, or have already arrived at my goal, but I press on to take hold of that for which Christ Jesus took hold of me. Brothers and sisters, I do not consider myself yet to have taken hold of it. But one thing I do: Forgetting what is behind and straining toward what is ahead, I press on toward the goal to win the prize for which God has called me heavenward in Christ Jesus. (Philippians 3:12-14)

I recently published a blog with a glaring error in the heading. However, I will put some of the blame on spell-check, a feature that can be both a blessing and a curse.

Have you ever sent a message, article, or written work only to discover an error or wrong word, as in my example above? Did the mistake make you blush or sweat? I find these experiences humbling and humiliating.

I'm not perfect. But oh, how I want to be! I know that I'm not alone in my struggle with perfectionism—setting higher standards for myself than I may be able to achieve. This trait can be a strength and a weakness, especially when it becomes a matter of pride.

As writers, perfectionism can produce stress, prevent us from sending our material to publishers, or cause us to miss deadlines.

Psalm 34:4 says, "I sought the LORD, and he answered me; he delivered me from all my fears." Let's strive for good, quality writing and ask for critiquing and editing by others; but ultimately, we need to ask the Lord to help us overcome our obsession with perfectionism.

PRAYER

Lord, I ask you to take away my need to be perfect. Only you, Lord, are perfect, and I know that you can help me manage this personal trait. Amen.

Let the Ink Flow

What impact is perfectionism having on your writing for better or for worse?

What are some steps you can take to help you cope with this tendency? Write them down.

Ego vs. Humility

Melony Teague

> Do nothing out of selfish ambition or vain conceit. Rather, in humility value others above yourselves, not looking to your own interests but each of you to the interests of the others. (Philippians 2:3-4)

It is assumed that writers have a certain amount of gumption, and with it comes ego; otherwise, they would not be doing what they do. Whether that is true in your case or not deserves a moment of reflection. There is nothing wrong with being grateful for the gifts that God has bestowed on you, and using them as you should. However, we have to be aware of our motives as writers. Are we writing for recognition from our peers, friends, and the fans out there? Are we climbing the literary ladder, so to speak, to get ahead? What exactly is it that motivates us to write?

It is good to be reminded that our first and foremost audience is God. With that in mind, we can see our work through the Lord's eyes. Let's purpose each day to let Jesus be our proofreader and editor in everything we work on, being careful not to fall into the trap of writing out of "selfish ambition or vain conceit."

This will be a testimony to our great Editor-in-Chief, the one who has given us the gift of writing.

PRAYER

Dear Jesus, rescue me from the trap of selfish ambition and vain conceit, and when I am tempted to feed my ego, teach me your way of humility so I may always lay my work before you. Amen.

Let the Ink Flow

The difference between humility and pride is not always obvious. When you examine the difference between humility and pride, does it affect how you view yourself in your writing or speaking life?

PROMPT

List some ways in which pride might cause you to stumble. Write about your thoughts as you reflect on this devotion and how it relates to you personally. Write about the emotions and thoughts it provoked in you.

Check Your Indicators

Melony Teague

In your relationships with one another, have the same mindset as Christ Jesus: Who, being in very nature God, did not consider equality with God something to be used to his own advantage. (Philippians 2:5-6)

When she was in kindergarten, the very first "Student of the Month" award that my daughter received was for fairness. We were so proud of her, but not at all surprised that her teacher had noticed a strong internal "indicator" that she had possessed from a young age. That little girl can still detect unfairness in any shape or form; it is on her radar. We have always counted on her to point out any unfair play or treatment among the six cousins. According to her, every child had to have the same quantity and size of candy; every child who wished to play had to take turns in a game. If this were not enforced, she was not afraid to let us know about it.

What are your indicators? What is it that sets off alarm bells in your heart? What character traits has God put in you that allow you to pick up on things that others might overlook? You can use this sensitivity to enhance your writing and enrich your life if you recognize your indicators as strengths. Perhaps even identifying that you have such indicators can bring understanding and a new revelation of how you can use them to be a better person and writer.

PRAYER

Dear Jesus, thank you that you have given me my own set of indicators. Help me to be aware of them, to use them as a tool and to be sensitive to issues around me that others may overlook. For your glory, reveal to me those traits that I have not recognized. Amen.

Let the Ink Flow

Identify your indicators, write them down, and think and pray about them.

Write a prayer to remind you to bring these indicators before the Lord each day. Print it out and post it in a prominent place.

Celebrating Individuality

Melony Teague

> For you created my inmost being; you knit me together in my mother's womb. I praise you because I am fearfully and wonderfully made; your works are wonderful, I know that full well. My frame was not hidden from you when I was made in the secret place, when I was woven together in the depths of the earth. (Psalm 139:13-15)

How-to books address the subject of finding your voice as a writer. A well-shaped piece sings out when it displays a writer's true-blue, confident voice. Have you ever considered that your testimony as a Christ follower is the clearest, most powerful voice that you have? Your own experiences cannot be challenged when you share how you have personally experienced God in your life.

We are to celebrate our individuality as those who have been "fearfully and wonderfully made." That part is not difficult to grasp, at least not on an intellectual level. When we look at children, we can see clearly that each one is unique. Do we apply this same standard to ourselves? We may feel inadequate, but God's grace through Jesus Christ's perfection lifts that burden. Knowing that we have a unique journey with our Lord is a liberating realization. Your own story, in a sense, is your voice to the world.

Revelation 12:11 says, "They triumphed over him by the blood of the Lamb and by the word of their testimony; they did not love their lives so much as to shrink from death." As you read this verse, consider how powerful your voice could be.

PRAYER

Dear Jesus, thank you for my own journey with you, for my unique voice that you have given to me. Help me always to recognize my testimony as a powerful weapon for your kingdom. Amen.

Let the Ink Flow

Are you comfortable with sharing your testimony? Why or why not?

Write about whatever may be hindering you in sharing your Christian testimony.

The Expressive One

Carol Ford

> He came to Simon Peter, who said to him, "Lord, are you going to wash my feet?" Jesus replied, "You do not realize now what I am doing, but later you will understand." "No," said Peter, "you shall never wash my feet." Jesus answered, "Unless I wash you, you have no part with me." "Then, Lord," Simon Peter replied, "not just my feet but my hands and my head as well!" (John 13:6-9)

Peter was the disciple who usually was the first to speak and act. On a personality test, Peter would probably score somewhere on the side of extroversion.

I can identify with Peter because I'm extroverted. I draw energy and stimulation from outside of myself, and I tend to be an external thinker, speaking my thoughts aloud. I am happiest when I can interact with other writers and discuss my ideas. Networking comes easily for me, and I can promote both my and others' accomplishments. Working alone for long periods of time can lower my energy level.

Yes, Peter had struggles with his impetuous behavior in speech and action, but we know how much Jesus loved Peter. This post-resurrection scene between Peter and Jesus shows that love:

> The third time he said to him, "Simon son of John, do you love me?" ... then [Jesus] said to him, "Follow me!" (John 21:17, 19b)

Peter's extroverted personality was a gift when he became God's spokesman after Christ's resurrection. You can read about this in Acts 2:14.

PRAYER

Dear Lord, thank you for my unique personality. Show me how to use my abilities to speak for you. Amen.

Let the Ink Flow

REFLECTION

There are many excellent online sites that discuss extroversion. These sites give practical ideas, techniques, and ways to use your preference effectively. Read through the traits and behaviors or take a free online test to see if this describes you.

PROMPT

Whether you are or aren't an extrovert, write below how an understanding of extroversion might help you, or others, with the skill of writing.

The Quiet One

Glenda Dekkema

> Moses said to the LORD, "Pardon your servant, LORD. I have never been eloquent, neither in the past nor since you have spoken to your servant. I am slow of speech and tongue." The LORD said to him, "Who gave human beings their mouths? Who makes them deaf or mute? Who gives them sight or makes them blind? Is it not I, the LORD? Now go; I will help you speak and will teach you what to say." (Exodus 4:10-12)

When I first started writing, I had these very thoughts: I am slow; I can't write well; I'm not very eloquent in face-to-face contact or even on the page. These thoughts led me to believe that others were better equipped for the task of public speaking and writing. My insecurities stemmed from the fear of failure or ridicule, or the belief that I didn't have the right personality for the job. However, my personality type—slightly introverted—and my preference for quiet reflection and feeling deeply have actually turned out to be an asset for the solitary life of writing.

Despite all this doubt I have had in the past, God kept tapping me on the shoulder, pointing to the computer, as if the Spirit were saying, "Get on with it!"

Do you ever wonder if you should give up on writing and start a new hobby—scrapbooking or hiking in the Himalayas by yourself? And, is writing a hobby? Or would you like it to be your full-time career, but believe it never will be because you don't believe you can do it? What is God calling you to do with your gift of writing?

PRAYER

Lord, thank you for being with me as I write. Give me the strength to overcome any doubt I may have in my abilities as a writer. You have given me my personality, and it is a gift. Amen.

Let the Ink Flow

If you identify with Moses, there are many excellent online sites that discuss introversion that you could research to help you. These sites give practical ideas, techniques, and ways to use your preference effectively.

PROMPT

Write about how an understanding of introversion might help you, or others, with the skill of writing.

Putting Our Talents to Work

Glenda Dekkema

> The man who had received five bags of gold went at once and put his money to work and gained five more. So also, the one with two bags gained two more. But the man who had received one bag went off, dug a hole in the ground and hid his master's money. (Matthew 25:16-18)

To the faithful servants who had received two and five bags of gold the master said, "Well done, good and faithful servant! You have been faithful with a few things; I will put you in charge of many things. Come and share your master's happiness" (Matthew 25:21,23). To the servant who buried his gold he said, "You wicked, lazy servant!" and then he ordered, "Throw that worthless servant outside, into the darkness, where there will be weeping and gnashing of teeth" (Matthew 25:26,30). This parable both inspires and scares me—for good reason!

When you read the excuses made by the servant with the one bag of gold, you could conclude that he was frightened, insecure, and believed that he was incapable of multiplying his money. Don't we sometimes feel this way? We'd rather lie low than sow; sleep rather than reap.

If we work earnestly to improve our skills and faithfully put ourselves out there with our writing, God will be pleased. Our Master will call us his good and faithful servants.

Do you have written work that is still hiding, like buried treasure, on your hard drive? With the Spirit's help, how can you rework it and use it to glorify God's kingdom?

PRAYER

Dear Lord, may I never be wasteful with this wonderful gift of writing that you have given to me. Help me to honor you with this gift and be faithful at every turn. Amen.

Let the Ink Flow

Read Matthew 25:14-30. Take some time to reflect on this parable.

PROMPT

Write about how you are investing your talents and how you might better use your talents.

Faithfulness

Blessings

Glenda Dekkema

> The LORD your God has blessed you in all the work of your hands. He has watched over your journey through this vast wilderness. These forty years the LORD your God has been with you, and you have not lacked anything. (Deuteronomy 2:7)

God is watching over everything we do and sees our struggles and our journey. Even though we might not experience the blessings as quickly as we would like, they will come.

When I first started writing, it felt as if I was working in a void, comparable to the Bible's version of "a vast wilderness." I was alone at my computer with very little feedback, and certainly not getting the high fives I longed for. But I trudged on through the wilderness with only a vision, basic talent, and a God who loves me.

Slowly the recognition trickled in. It started out with a few unpaid, published articles, and then a few short feature paid articles, and then longer articles, then a column, a few books, and finally a full-time job as a writer. Although it didn't take forty years, it certainly felt like it did!

PRAYER

Dear Lord, help us to use our talents as writers and to be patient in all we do. Remind us that our work will be blessed. Amen.

Let the Ink Flow

Take some time to reflect on the ways that God has blessed your writing career.

Write down some ways in which you see God's blessings in your life and work.

Forty

Carol Ford

> The LORD then said to Noah, "Go into the ark, you and your whole family, because I have found you righteous in this generation. . . . Seven days from now I will send rain on the earth for forty days and forty nights." (Genesis 7:1,4a)

My husband and I recently celebrated our fortieth wedding anniversary. It seemed like such a milestone in our marriage, especially in today's culture. From my experience, a marriage requires perseverance through struggles, a large dose of acceptance and grace for each other's faults, and a complete commitment to our promise before God and witnesses.

Forty is also a prevalent and significant number used throughout Scripture. I did an online search—"forty years in Scripture"—and I was amazed at the list of events and references I found. One site mentioned that the number forty shows up 146 times in Scripture, and it usually symbolizes trial, testing, or probation. Some references that stand out are the forty days of the flood, Moses' forty days on Mount Sinai, Israel's forty years wandering in the wilderness, and Jesus' forty days of temptation.[1]

What can writers learn from these biblical events? Writing can have its highs and lows, and sometimes we might feel like Noah did; we are writing when no one else can see the purpose. Or we are speaking or writing something that God has given us, but others don't want to hear it. We may experience the temptation to want all the recognition instead of giving God the glory. Can we persevere even on the days when there is no inspiration or acceptance, or when we receive rejections and critical feedback? Let's remember that we are not writing for ourselves, but rather to carry forward our promise to God in sharing his Word.

PRAYER

Lord, remind us once again of the need to stay faithful and committed to what you want us to write. Amen.

Let the Ink Flow

What writing milestone can you celebrate today?

Write a praise piece thanking God for your talent and skills.

1. "Meaning of Numbers in the Bible: The Number 40" (http://www.
biblestudy.org/bibleref/meaning-of-numbers-in-bible/40.html).

Give Them Something to Eat

Melony Teague

As evening approached, the disciples came to him and said, "This is
a remote place, and it's already getting late. Send the crowds away,
so they can go to the villages and buy themselves some food." Jesus
replied, "They do not need to go away. You give them something to eat."
"We have here only five loaves of bread and two fish," they answered.
"Bring them here to me," he said. (Matthew 14:15-18)

Have you ever considered yourself as "one who feeds"—in this case,
one who assists with feeding? Ultimately, Jesus is the one who feeds
us, but he has asked us to do as he did. Let's consider the words
we write as food for the soul. As writers and speakers, we have the
means to inspire and uplift those who read our words. When we
write, we reach a place in the reader's hearts that might not otherwise be touched.

Let our words be full of substance so that none go away hungry.
Let them be filled to overflowing so there is plenty for everyone.
Jesus instructed, "Bring them here to me." Let us do so by the words
that we choose to place within our word count.

If you haven't previously recognized this privilege and responsibility, take a few moments to reflect on how your words, inspired by
your faith in Christ, go out just like loaves to the hungry. You may
feel as if you have little to offer, but with God, five loaves and two
fish became a feast for thousands. In the same way, as you offer what
you have to God, the Lord will use it to inspire, feed, and nourish the
souls of those hungry for words of substance.

PRAYER

Dear Jesus, watch over every word I write so I may see it as loaves
and fish in your hands. Take what I have and make it yours so others may be nourished and be encouraged. Help me to always bring
those in need to you in prayer, to be fed and cared for by you. Please
feed and take care of me too. Thank you for the privilege of being a
writer, for the power of words that you have entrusted to me. Amen.

Let the Ink Flow

Take a few moments to reflect on your role as a Christian writer who has a part in "feeding the hungry" through your work. How seriously do you take this? How will it affect the way you'll approach your work in the future?

PROMPT

Write about how you might best offer your writing to feed others. If it feels right to you, write a letter to God committing your writing or speaking for this purpose.

Full Armor of God

Glenda Dekkema

> Now the serpent was more crafty than any of the wild animals the LORD God had made. He said to the woman, "Did God really say, 'You must not eat from the tree in the garden'?" (Genesis 3:1)

C. S. Lewis's book *The Screwtape Letters* frightened me as a teenager—probably a good thing—and it still sticks with me today. Screwtape, the highly experienced serpent, wrote thirty-one letters to Wormwood, the novice, on how to undermine a human being's Christian faith by using several devious ways. The tactics are brilliant, subtle, and crafty. The saboteur has many different forms. He might be our inner critic and/or he can come in the form of relationship, financial, emotional, and health distractions. He knows where we are most vulnerable, and that is where he decides to have a picnic—if you let him.

Luke 4:13 tells us about the temptation of Jesus: "When the devil had finished all this tempting, he left him." Phew! That's good, right? Jesus won. But then the verse adds, "until an opportune time." That slimy devil!

If we are to defeat Satan's cunning attempts to destroy anything good we are trying to do, we must, as the apostle Paul says, put on the full armor of God: "Finally, be strong in the Lord and in his mighty power. Put on the full armor of God, so that you can take your stand against the devil's schemes" (Ephesians 6:10-11).

PRAYER

Dear Lord, help me to wear the armor of truth, righteousness, peace, faith, and salvation, and to be strong in the power of the Holy Spirit. Amen.

Let the Ink Flow

Read Ephesians 6:10-20. What does the metaphor of armor mean to you today?

Write about practical methods that you can use to put on the full armor of God.

Be Still

Glenda Dekkema

Be still, and know that I am God. (Psalm 46:10)

Once upon a time, there was a professor who went to visit a wise old monk. As soon as the professor sat down on his cushion, he started to talk, sharing his vast knowledge in a long, windy monologue. The monk listened patiently. Then the monk silently poured some tea from a large teapot into a tiny cup. While the professor continued to talk, the monk continued to pour. Soon, the tea was overflowing the teacup and running all over the floor. And the monk continued to pour. The professor was aghast. He stopped his monologue, stood up, and yelled at the monk, asking him why he didn't watch what he was doing. The monk responded, "This cup is like your mind. It can't take in anything because it is already full."

Writing is like talking. We are pouring out the words after shaping, carving, and chiseling them. We are told to read and, yes, we do—a lot. We fill our minds and pour more onto the paper. We keep pouring.

There is a time to silence our mouths, minds, and pens—to empty ourselves so that we are able to receive whatever it is that God wants to give us. To bask in the presence of God, we don't need any words. Just be. Still.

PRAYER

Dear Lord, help us to be still and know that you are God. Amen.

Let the Ink Flow

Have you ever entered a silent prayer? One way to start one is simply to say, "Here I am, Lord."

This is the only prompt that will challenge you *not* to write. Go to a place of solitude, whether it is your porch, or a walk in the forest, or your bathroom—if you can't get away anywhere. Breathe deeply. Choose one word only, and repeat that word on the inhalation. I like to use the word "peace," but you may choose any word that strengthens you. Do this for five minutes so that you can empty your mind. Don't think. Just feel.

To God Be the Glory

Claudia Loopstra

You yourselves are our letter, written on our hearts, known and read by everyone. You show that you are a letter from Christ, the result of our ministry, written not with ink but with the Spirit of the living God, not on tablets of stone but on tablets of human hearts. (2 Corinthians 3:2-3)

In Paul's message to the Corinthians he commended them for being living letters from Christ. In other words, their outward behavior demonstrated their faith as they actively implemented their belief in him by how they lived. God used the apostle Paul, as well as the other disciples, to be followers of Jesus. Their behavior reflected that Christ was at the core of their being.

I am reminded that our gifts and capabilities are imparted to us by our heavenly Father. As we write, let us remember that God has given us our talent. We write not only with ink, but also with our hearts as the Holy Spirit guides us.

To God be the glory, great things He hath done;
So loved He the world that He gave us His Son,
Who yielded His life an atonement for sin,
And opened the life gate that all may go in.[1]

PRAYER

Dear Lord, let me never lose sight of the fact that it is you who breathed life into me through the Holy Spirit. May my commitment to you be as a letter written on my heart, and may my writing indicate that I write not only with ink but also with the Spirit of the living God working within. Amen.

Let the Ink Flow

Each time you sit down before the blank page, take a few minutes and give thanks that the Holy Spirit uses your talent to glorify God.

PROMPT

Write out your prayer of thanksgiving on an index card and leave it on your desk beside your computer. If you have a journal, make a note of how the Holy Spirit is directing your writing; then give God the glory with prayerful thanksgiving.

NOTES

1. Lyrics by Fanny Crosby, 1875.

True Value

Glenda Dekkema

But godliness with contentment is great gain. For we brought nothing into the world, and we can take nothing out of it. But if we have food and clothing, we will be content with that. Those who want to get rich fall into temptation and a trap and into many foolish and harmful desires that plunge people into ruin and destruction. For the love of money is a root of all kinds of evil. Some people, eager for money, have wandered from the faith and pierced themselves with many griefs. (1 Timothy 6:6-10)

I once took a course called "Accelerated Program for Six-Figure Copywriting." I was interested in the six figures—copywriting, not so much. Should the need for money determine how we employ our writing abilities?

As Christian writers, should we worry about food, clothing, and housing? How do we measure true value? Is it through money or through following what God wants us to do? At what point do we have enough money to be comfortable?

The Bible talks a lot about greed—we certainly don't want to embrace greed by—metaphorically speaking—drinking champagne and eating caviar in that back alley. The Bible also talks about the birds of the air, how they neither sow nor reap, and yet our heavenly Father feeds them.

If we can match our livelihood with what we love to do, then we will be using our God-given talents. "Godliness with contentment is great gain." We really don't need the six figures.

PRAYER

Dear Lord, help me to find the right balance between the need for money to pay for my basic needs and the need to pursue my passion to write. Amen.

Let the Ink Flow

If you didn't have to earn money, what would you choose to do with the rest of your life?

Write about whether you would continue to do what you are doing right now. Explain why.

Christian Writer

Glenda Dekkema

> With this in mind, we constantly pray for you, that our God may make
> you worthy of his calling, and that by his power he may bring to fruition
> your every desire for goodness and your every deed prompted by faith.
> We pray this so that the name of our Lord Jesus may be glorified in you,
> and you in him, according to the grace of our God and the Lord Jesus
> Christ. (2 Thessalonians 1:11-12)

To quote Dave Barry: "The problem with writing about religion is
that you run the risk of offending sincerely religious people, and then
they come after you with machetes."[1]

It can be daunting to be a Christian writer. How do we know
for sure that what we say is considered to be biblically correct? Are
we certain that we haven't offended our Christian readers with our
interpretation of the Holy Scriptures? Have we pleased God with our
words? Do we need a PhD in Hebrew or Greek in order to be able to
say anything at all about how the Bible inspires us to live?

This fear of offending other Christians shouldn't prevent us from
doing what we are called to do. But, we should always pray that God
will keep us on the right track—Christ's track—in our writing.

PRAYER

Dear Lord, may the words of my mouth and everything that I write
be pleasing to you. Amen.

Let the Ink Flow

Do you think it is daunting to be a Christian writer? Why or why not?

PROMPT

Write down what frightens you or doesn't frighten you about being a Christian writer.

NOTES

1. http://www.brainyquote.com/search_results.html?q=machetes.

Faith Works

Glenda Dekkema

> In the same way, faith by itself, if it is not accompanied by action, is dead. But someone will say, "You have faith; I have deeds." Show me your faith without deeds, and I will show you my faith by my deeds. You believe that there is one God. Good! Even the demons believe that—and shudder. (James 2:17-19)

During the WWII Nazi occupation of Holland, Aafko, my grandfather-in-law, was a member of the Dutch resistance. The Nazis ordered Aafko to round up the Jews in his neighborhood to be sent to concentration camps and possibly eventual extermination. Putting his own life at stake, Aafko warned these Jews to flee. A Dutch citizen informed the Nazis of Aafko's actions. For this, Aafko was captured and imprisoned. He was later shot along with hundreds of other prisoners—execution style—and he was thrown into a mass grave. He was only thirty-six years old.

After the war, the mass grave was excavated so that the war victims buried there could receive a proper funeral. In Aafko's coat pocket was a small Bible with the following page earmarked: "For I am convinced that neither death nor life, neither angels nor demons, neither the present nor the future, nor any powers, neither height nor depth, nor anything else in all creation, will be able to separate us from the love of God that is in Christ Jesus our Lord" (Romans 8:38-39).

Aafko was never given the opportunity to tell us about his faith. Through his actions, he was able to show us—from beyond the grave—what kind of a man he was, and the faith that he held dear to his heart. Through Aafko's powerful acts of faith, I believe that I know him. Now that you have read this story, you know him too.

PRAYER

Lord, may our deeds—in how we tell our stories—reveal our faith. Amen.

Let the Ink Flow

Take a moment to reflect on the faithful who have gone before us. How would you describe faith in action?

PROMPT

Write a story or memoir to depict such faith in action.

Well Done

Glenda Dekkema

> Then you will call, and the LORD will answer; you will cry for help, and he
> will say: Here am I. The LORD will guide you always; he will satisfy your
> needs in a sun-scorched land and will strengthen your frame. You will
> be like a well-watered garden, like a spring whose waters never fail.
> (Isaiah 58:9a,11)

If you never become rich or famous through your writing, will you still be satisfied with God's praise?

Dorene Meyer's short story "On Writing with Passion and Integrity" is published in the anthology *Hot Apple Cider*. During a leap of faith, she quit her day job to take on the challenging task of becoming a full-time writer, with little or no pay and rare recognition. She said, "I feel God's presence with me as I write."[1]

After I became a mother, I gave up my nursing career, stayed at home, and wrote. I had no idea if I would ever be successful at it. I just thought that it would be fun to do while the kids took naps. Once I got into it, I fairly quickly realized that God might be calling me to this profession—and that he could use me.

Eventually my registered nurse status expired, and my marriage failed, forcing me to rely solely on my writing for an income. It was a scary time because not only was I afraid of poverty, but also I feared the humiliation that comes with failing at something that I was pouring my heart and soul into.

God gave me strength to keep going by putting encouraging people in my path, and gave me the determination to keep going by convincing me that I was doing God's will. As you've already heard, this story has a happy ending. I got a job as a full-time Christian writer!

PRAYER

Lord, I know that if I do your will, you will satisfy my needs. You will strengthen me. I will be like a well-watered garden, like a spring whose waters never fail. Thank you, Lord. Amen.

Let the Ink Flow

REFLECTION

Is it enough for you to have God's approval? Why or why not?

PROMPT

Write out a two-page prayer to God declaring your intentions.

NOTES

1. Dorene Meyer, "On Writing with Passion and Integrity," in *Hot Apple Cider: Words to Stir the Heart and Warm the Soul*, ed. N. J. Lindquist and Wendy Elaine Nelles (Markham, ON: That's Life! Communications, 2008), 251. Since this story was published, Dorene Meyer has become a prolific and award-winning Canadian author.

Writing with Love

Glenda Dekkema

> Love is patient, love is kind. It does not envy, it does not boast, it is not proud. It does not dishonor others, it is not self-seeking, it is not easily angered, it keeps no record of wrongs. Love does not delight in evil but rejoices with the truth. It always protects, always trusts, always hopes, always perseveres. (1 Corinthians 13:4-7)

Recently, in preparation for *As the Ink Flows*, I wondered how this text would sound if we substituted "writing" for "love." Please do this with me, because you'll see how fitting it is.

> *Writing* is patient, *writing* is kind. It does not envy, it does not boast, it is not proud. It does not dishonor others, it is not self-seeking, it is not easily angered, it keeps no record of wrongs. *Writing* does not delight in evil but rejoices with the truth. It always protects, always trusts, always hopes, always perseveres.

Imagine how much love we could spread with our writing if we followed this advice! How much healing could we bring to this world? How many relationships could we restore through our choice of words? Sometimes it can be as simple as changing a single word in our text. Let's choose our words wisely and lovingly.

PRAYER

Dear Lord, help me to use your description of perfect love as a guide on how to write with love. Amen.

Let the Ink Flow

Mother Teresa said, "I'm a little pencil in the hand of a writing God, who is sending a love letter to the world." Reflect on what this means to you.

PROMPT

Write a love letter to the world, the army, a victim, or your nemesis. Use the words of 1 Corinthians 13:4-7 to guide you.

Curbing the Urge

Melony Teague

> Likewise, the tongue is a small part of the body, but it makes great boasts. Consider what a great forest is set on fire by a small spark. The tongue also is a fire, a world of evil among the parts of the body. It corrupts the whole body, sets the whole course of one's life on fire, and is itself set on fire by hell. (James 3:3-6)

We see a prevailing culture all around us that is dedicated to venting frustration and indignation. It is easy to give in to the urge to vent when life presents you with circumstances that could be fodder for a passionate sharing of one's opinion. The tongue is that little organ we are called upon to master.

I have let the angry words flow onto the page when I've needed to blow off steam as a result of an unpleasant event. As soon as I set my pen down, I felt as if a burden was lifted. If the words were intended for my eyes only, as therapeutic journaling, little harm was done. When words are intended for publication, however, more care must be taken.

James warns us that a small spark can set ablaze a roaring fire that may burn out of control. Our written words can cause the same sort of situation.

It's the responsibility of Christian writers to set a higher standard and curb the urge to lash out with the pen. Whether or not we are justified in what we mean to convey is not the point. Take a deep breath. Look at the situation objectively. Ask yourself, "How can I write about this situation in a way that brings awareness, healing, and growth?"

PRAYER

Dear Jesus, forgive me for times when I have let my emotions get the better of me. When I feel wronged and am tempted to vent on the page, give me the grace to step back and turn my angry words into words that give life rather than take it away. Amen.

Let the Ink Flow

How do you express yourself when you are emotionally charged?

Do you journal? If you do, how can journaling help you process your emotions and tame your tongue? If you don't journal, write out some ideas on how you think it could help you to process your emotions and tame your tongue. Write about your thoughts and attitude toward journaling.

Dig Deeper

Melony Teague

The fear of the LORD is the beginning of wisdom; all who follow his precepts have good understanding. To him belongs eternal praise. (Psalm 111:10)

Sometimes heart-wrenching things happen. We weep with the brokenhearted. The question inevitably arises: "Why did this happen?"

Author and pastor Rick Warren is well-known for writing *The Purpose Driven Life: What on Earth Am I Here For?* After the suicide death of his son, Matthew, he tweeted: "I don't have to know why everything happens since I know God is Good, he loves me, life on earth isn't the whole story."

Mental illness played a role in this young man's life, and everything had been done to help. Days later Rick tweeted this: "Someone on the Internet sold Matthew an unregistered gun. I pray he seeks God's forgiveness. I forgive him."[1]

As I read those words, I sat stunned. They spoke more to me than all the books that Rick Warren wrote. I realized that the way I live my Christian life speaks volumes about who I am and whom I serve, much louder than any words I write or speak. Are the words that I write and speak aligned with the story that my life conveys to others? The kind of forgiveness offered by Rick under these circumstances can come only from a real and personal understanding of what Christ did for us.

Before you put pen to paper, seek wisdom, knowledge, and understanding from the Lord to share authentic words with others.

PRAYER

Dear Jesus, when I don't comprehend, help me to seek understanding from you before all others. Amen.

Let the Ink Flow

In what circumstance in your life has God revealed divine wisdom and understanding?

Write about that experience and what you learned from it.

1. Rick Warren (@RickWarren) April 11, 2013 (https://twitter.comRick Warren/status/322434892828917760).

Judging Your Cover

Melony Teague

> They said, "Is this not Jesus, the son of Joseph, whose father and
> mother we know? How can he now say, 'I came down from heaven'?"
> (John 6:42)

Let's face it: despite the proverbial warning to the contrary, quite often a book *is* judged by its cover. Otherwise, cover designers would be out of a job! Much time is spent on the plan for a book's cover. If you're like me, when you go to the bookstore, you are drawn to the nicest covers. It is disappointing to pick up a book that promises a wonderful story, only to find that what you had expected is not there.

In the same way, the world looks at us as a book that contains a story. The sad thing is that often our outside doesn't portray what is inside.

Jesus knew what it felt like to be judged by outward appearances (John 6:42) and not by who he really was. He was seen as a carpenter, and yet he was so much more: "Yet for us there is but one God, the Father, from whom all things came and for whom we live; and there is but one Lord, Jesus Christ, through whom all things came and through whom we live" (1 Corinthians 8:6).

If we consider the mystery of our transformation through Christ, we should be more open to share our personal faith with those around us. Are you being honest about your faith experience? Our cover can be the best way to bring someone to Christ, particularly as a witness to those who would never set foot in a traditional church.

Readers prefer authenticity to polished, fake perfectionism. There is no shame in being wisely real and honest; we have an esteemed coauthor whose name should be displayed on our cover. His name is Jesus Christ.

PRAYER

Dear Jesus, help me to develop my life cover as a beautiful reflection of the miraculous wonder of transformation occurring, through you, within my heart. Amen.

Let the Ink Flow

REFLECTION

If you were to design a book cover reflecting your life with Christ, what would it look like?

PROMPT

Are you able to see Christ as your coauthor, or do you struggle to see the one who is writing your story with you? Write about it.

Where Two or Three Gather

Melony Teague

> "Again, truly I tell you that if two of you on earth agree about any-
> thing they ask for, it will be done for them by my Father in heaven.
> For where two or three gather in my name, there am I with them."
> (Matthew 18:19-20)

How many times have we read or heard these verses from Matthew? If Jesus actually appeared in our midst the way he did to his followers after his resurrection, what would your reaction be? These verses challenge us to examine whether we truly do believe that wherever we gather as Christ's followers, he is there, among us. Will our speech and behavior be different if this truth has sunk in?

If your writing were being read over your shoulder by Jesus, would you write in the same way? Why or why not?

When we gather as part of a group of writers who belong to him, in what ways do we acknowledge Christ's presence? Grasping the powerful truth of his presence in a real way, and agreeing to do something in his name, what wonderful things might happen?

PRAYER

Dear Jesus, help me to understand what it means to have you actually among us. When I forget to acknowledge you, please forgive me. Open my mind and my heart to sense, in an undeniable way, the power of your presence. Amen.

Let the Ink Flow

Take some time to reflect on the questions posed in today's devotion. What picture is forming in your mind of how we exclude Jesus from what we are doing?

PROMPT

Jot down some ways you can invite Jesus into your writing today.

Stand Firm in Love

Melony Teague

> Be on your guard; stand firm in the faith; be courageous; be strong.
> Do everything in love. (1 Corinthians 16:13-14)

Sometimes, things need to be said. As ambassadors of Christ, we are to be salt and light in the world (Matthew 5:13-16). We are to speak for those who have no voice. Let's face it: this task is not always comfortable.

We are encouraged to watch and stand fast in the faith, not allowing ourselves to become timid in the face of opposition or criticism. In our zeal we stand firm in the face of adversity, but we may forget about verse 14, which reminds us, "Do everything in love." Love, as you know, is patient and kind, is not boastful, and puts others above self (1 Corinthians 13:4-5). Jesus Christ is a wonderful example. He said things that upset people, but he did so with love and with insight. Sadly lacking today is a willingness to stand firm in what we believe is right by Jesus' standards. Afraid to offend or to upset anyone, we use our best euphemisms to express the message we want to convey.

I pray that we endeavor to stand firm in love. Let us also keep our passion for what is right at a simmer. Let us be ready to bring soothing words to those who are cold and weary. For persons looking for a good dose of truth, let us be among those who are ready to pour ourselves out to share that truth, regardless of our fears.

PRAYER

Dear Jesus, when I don't feel at all brave but need to speak the truth, remind me that you are there. Keep me mindful of your indescribable love for me and for my readers. Give me the strength I need to stand up for those who have no voice and to love those who wish to turn a deaf ear. It is only through you that I am able to face it all with courage. Thank you for your promise that you'll never leave or forsake me. Amen.

Let the Ink Flow

REFLECTION

Think about an issue that gets you easily riled up. Knowing that God loves unconditionally, consider how you can address an issue that is "hot" and do so with love at the same time.

PROMPT

Take a moment to write about the issue in the most loving and compassionate way you can, yet without compromise. Before you begin, pray. Ask Jesus to help you see the situation through his eyes.

He Loves Me,
He Loves Me Not

Melony Teague

> For I am convinced that neither death nor life, neither angels nor
> demons, neither the present nor the future, nor any powers, neither
> height nor depth, nor anything else in all creation, will be able to
> separate us from the love of God that is in Christ Jesus our Lord.
> (Romans 8:38-39)

"He loves me, he loves me not," or maybe it's, "She loves me, she loves me not," as daisy petals fall to the ground. Not a very reliable way of telling if we are truly loved, is it? Yet sometimes this is exactly what we think of God. We think: *I messed up today.* "He loves me not." Or, *I did good things today. I'm sure that God is pleased with me.* "He loves me."

Do we really think that God's opinion of us changes so easily? When we put it that way, it sounds absurd. Honestly, aren't we just a little bit resistant to the fact that God loves us no matter what we do or do not do? How we feel about ourselves will impact our writing.

No matter how many times we fail, or how many rejection letters we receive, God's unmerited favor rests on us. We know this in our heads, but do we at times fall into the trap of feeling that we need to earn God's love? In Romans 8 we're reminded that nothing can separate us from the love of God. Sometimes it's difficult to accept that in a personal way. It's easy to think that Jesus came to save the world—but did he really come for *me*?

PRAYER

Dear Jesus, help me not to fall into the daisy-petal way of thinking about your love. May my heart always know and accept that your love for me is unconditional. Thank you. Help me to share that love with others. Amen.

Let the Ink Flow

Identify the thoughts that perhaps make it hard for you to believe that God's love extends to you in a personal and real way. What lies have you believed about how God sees you?

Write a paragraph or a poem about God's unconditional and personal love for you. Write about the lies that trip us up in our acceptance of love from God and from others. Write about your own ability to love yourself.

Nonverbal Communication

Melony Teague

> The heavens declare the glory of God; the skies proclaim the work of his hands. Day after day they pour forth speech; night after night they reveal knowledge. They have no speech, they use no words; no sound is heard from them. Yet their voice goes out into all the earth, their words to the ends of the world. . . . May these words of my mouth and this meditation of my heart be pleasing in your sight, LORD, my Rock and my Redeemer. (Psalm 19:1-4,14)

In Psalm 19 the psalmist talks about how the heavens declare the glory of God. He describes how the sun and the heavens silently speak of God's greatness and reveal knowledge. The psalm concludes with the psalmist's appeal to God. He is concerned with the words of his mouth and the thoughts of his innermost being. His desire is to be pleasing in the sight of the great Creator.

The heavens are silently shouting out the wonders of God in their beauty and the mysteries within the cosmos. Just because these "words" are silent, they are no less heard. It is easy to focus on the words that we write and say, yet forget about the meditation of our hearts that may never be uttered. What we *do not* say can sometimes speak more loudly than what we *do* say.

Just as the heavens communicate a silent ode to their Creator, so can we, as God's handiwork. What we are, in essence, speaks more loudly than what we communicate with words. Children pick up on this easily and see past what we say to what we do and who we are. Shouldn't our prayer imitate that of the psalmist in asking that his thoughts be pleasing to his Rock and Redeemer?

PRAYER

Dear Jesus, my Rock and my Redeemer, as the heavens declare your majesty, so do I want to reflect your glory in all that I say and do. Help me to be mindful of what I communicate without speaking. In the psalmist's prayer, I ask, "May these words of my mouth and this meditation of my heart be pleasing in your sight." Amen.

Let the Ink Flow

Meditate on the text in today's devotion.

Write your own psalm or song below with the focus on expressing praise as discussed in this devotion.

I Know God Can

Glenda Dekkema

> But Moses said, "Pardon your servant, LORD. Please send someone else." Then the LORD's anger burned against Moses and he said, "What about your brother, Aaron the Levite? I know he can speak well. He is already on his way to meet you, and he will be glad to see you. You shall speak to him and put words in his mouth; I will help both of you speak and will teach you what to do." (Exodus 4:13-15)

As writers, we may need to team up with experts to help us. This could be through a writers' group, courses, books, a coach, and definitely an editor. By the way, writing anything without an editor is like going to court without a lawyer.

In the classic children's storybook *The Little Engine That Could*, as retold by Watty Piper, the little steam engine has a heavy load to pull and a steep hill to climb. She tries to do it by herself, but can't. She asks for help from others but faces repeated rejection, until she finally asks for assistance from another little steam engine. They work cooperatively while reciting, "I think I can, I think I can, I think I can." Finally, after a lot of hard work, the two of them successfully make it up the steep hill, using their combined perseverance and belief. Whoever said that everything we needed to know we learned in kindergarten might well be right!

It is interesting that it is another little steam engine—about the same size as the little engine herself is—who helps her.

Let's work with other Christians, call on God to help us, and repeat, "I know God can, I know God can, I know God can."

PRAYER

I know you can. Thank you, Lord. Amen.

Let the Ink Flow

Is there someone you trust who can help you? Who is this person, and why do you trust him or her?

If you already have people helping you in your writing career, write about when you got to know them and how and why they started to help you. If you don't have anyone helping you at the moment, write out a game plan for how you will team up with someone.

Getting Dirty in the Valley

Melony Teague

> The hand of the LORD was on me, and he brought me out by the Spirit
> of the LORD and set me in the middle of a valley; it was full of bones.
> He led me back and forth among them, and I saw a great many bones
> on the floor of the valley, bones that were very dry. He asked me, "Son
> of man, can these bones live?" I said, "Sovereign LORD, you alone know."
> (Ezekiel 37:1-3)

Sometimes what God calls us to address as writers is not all about
blessings and warm fuzzy feelings. We are required to tackle subject
matter that reeks of death and destruction. It is not at all pleasant.
At times we are called to face a valley of dry, dead bones. It is tempting to do our best Jonah impersonation and head for safer ground.
Jonah headed in the opposite direction and ran away from the Lord
and did not do what he was told by God to do because he had his
own reasons why Nineveh was not on his list of preferred destina-
tions (Jonah 1:3).

It is far nicer to write about the glory moments and the moun-
taintop experiences. Yet, it is in the valley, among those who seem to
be dead, that God can teach, bring life, and show us truth. In those
uncomfortable situations, when we stand face to face with the stark
reality of our limitations, we can turn to the one who can breathe
life into them. We may have to expose and shine truth and light onto
a subject that we would rather avoid. Whatever it may be, as you
bravely tackle it with God's guidance, understand that God is the
sovereign Lord who knows it all.

PRAYER

Dear Jesus, when I face the uncomfortable, unlovely things in life,
guide my words and deeds so you can breathe life through me into
the death and decay in society. I want to resist the urge to flee like
Jonah. Help me, instead, to treasure the privilege, honor, and responsibility of being a writer who fears you above all. Amen.

Let the Ink Flow

When have you taken the "Jonah route" in your writing?

Write about how taking this approach made you feel.

Tears

Carol Ford

> For God did not send his Son into the world to condemn the world, but to save the world through him. Whoever believes in him is not condemned, but whoever does not believe stands condemned already because they have not believed in the name of God's one and only Son. (John 3:17-18)

Today the wind was blowing the rain against our patio doors. As I watched the slow descent of drops on the window, it reminded me of tears. I felt sadness in my heart for a world that has turned away from God. It's God's world, but so many do not know Jesus as their personal savior. People seem indifferent, distracted, and negligent of his offer of eternal life.

One day we will be accountable. Romans 14:11-12 says, "'As surely as I live,' says the Lord, 'every knee will bow before me; every tongue will acknowledge God.'" So then, each of us will give an account of ourselves to God. What am I doing to show others how to find forgiveness, peace, and salvation before that day?

These sobering thoughts help me realize the importance of my writing and speaking. As Christian writers, we have an opportunity and responsibility to direct the world's attention toward our Savior. I want to use my gifts for this purpose.

PRAYER

Today, Lord, help me to remember how important it is to use my writing to share your wonderful gift of salvation. Amen.

Let the Ink Flow

Have you written or spoken to anyone in the last week about God's plan of salvation? Why or why not?

PROMPT

If someone were to ask you how to get to heaven, what would you say? Write a reply in two or three sentences.

Répondez, S'il Vous Plaît

Melony Teague

> So they took the bull given them and prepared it. Then they called
> on the name of Baal from morning till noon. "Baal, answer us!" they
> shouted. But there was no response; no one answered. And they
> danced around the altar they had made. . . . Midday passed, and they
> continued their frantic prophesying until the time for the evening
> sacrifice. But there was no response, no one answered, no one paid
> attention. (1 Kings 18:26,29)

When invitations are sent out for an event, usually guests are expected to RSVP. This enables the host to prepare for the event and make sure there is enough food for all the guests. In some instances, if you have not responded and been added to the official guest list, you will not be permitted to attend.

In the Scripture verses above we see an example of a response, or in this case, the lack of response from Baal. In the book of Daniel we read how Daniel prayed, God heard, God responded, and the angel was dispatched. Now read Daniel 10:12.

It would be beneficial to consider how a response or lack thereof can play an important part in our own relationships. It may be surprising to you that God responded to Daniel in a very direct and personal way. Do you believe that the Lord can and will respond to your heart? How wonderful to think that your Creator is there to RSVP when you extend the invitation!

God has sent out a personal invitation for a close relationship with us in the form of his only Son, Jesus. It is up to us to RSVP. Having responded, "Yes," don't we want to share this invitation with others through our writing?

PRAYER

Dear Jesus, thank you for your personal response to me. Help me to remember that responses are an important part of my spiritual life. Amen.

Let the Ink Flow

Consider memorizing Daniel 10:12 in order to remember that God responds to the heart. How do you respond to God's unfailing love?

PROMPT

Write about how God responds to your heart, prayers, and needs. Knowing that God loves you, write about your own heartfelt response to God.

About the Authors

GLENDA DEKKEMA is a full-time writer for Christian Blind Mission. In the past she wrote the chaplaincy column for *Senior Care Canada* magazine. Her non-fiction articles—focused on health, the environment, family life, and humor—are published in magazines and newspapers in Canada and Europe. She is a professional member of The Word Guild, Canada's largest Christian organization for writers. Glenda loves to tell stories, but she especially enjoys listening to her friends telling them while she laughs or cries over a few cups of coffee.

www.glendadekkema.com

MELONY TEAGUE was born in South Africa and im-migrated to Canada in 1999. She lives in Toronto with her husband and their two children. She is a freelance writer who believes that everyone has a story to tell, and each story is unique and sometimes wilder than fiction. She loves to uncover the good news in society and writes human interest and com-munity pieces. Melony has contributed columns and community articles for the local media over the years. Melony's guest columns address issues pertaining to the life and health of her community. She loves to inspire and motivate others through her written words. She is also a ghostwriter and biographer and handles communications and public relations for two nonprofit missions or-ganizations in Canada. She reviews Christian fiction on her website and is an active member of The Word Guild and InScribe Christian Writers' Fellowship.

www.melonyteague.com

CAROL FORD is writing a memoir about her adoption and birth family reunion at the age of fifty. She's an active member of The Word Guild, and her fictional short story about elder abuse was a finalist in its 2013 Fresh Ink Contest. Another short story, "My Mother's Gift," is published in *Hot Apple Cider with Cinnamon*. Carol facilitates a local Christian writers' group in her home. She is certified in MBTI (Myers Briggs Type Indicator) and Life Skills Coaching and offers consulting, specializing in personality assessments, communication, and career management. She shares her work experience weekly on Hope Stream Radio and speaks at church, college, industry, and community events. Carol and her husband live in Newmarket, Ontario.

http://carolfordassociates.wordpress.com

CLAUDIA LOOPSTRA is a wife, a mother of two, a grandmother of six, and an author. She has recently completed her memoir, *Redemptive Love: Living with an Alcoholic Father*. Claudia has had several short stories and articles published. In addition to giving seminars on the topics "Strengthening Your Devotional Life" and "Emotional and Physical Abuse and Forgiveness," Claudia has delivered topical speeches on prayer and grief. She was a bereavement facilitator for approximately ten years. During the 1990s, Claudia served on the National Executive of Women Alive. She is currently a member of The Word Guild.

www.claudialoopstra.com

MARGUERITE CUMMINGS has a distinctively international background. Born in Belgium into a French-speaking family with roots in Austria, Belgium, Poland, and Romania, she moved to England in her late teens. There she completed an Oxford degree, attended Bible college, trained as a technical writer and editor, and worked in computing, until her move to Canada in 1998. Marguerite has been a member of The Word Guild since 2006. She contributed the article "O Canada" to the bestselling Canadian anthology *A Second Cup of Hot Apple Cider* (2011), and received an Award of Merit in 2012 for this story. She continued her involvement with the Hot Apple Cider Books series by designing two reader's guides, coediting two discussion guides, and contributing to *Hot Apple Cider with Cinnamon* (2015). She is looking forward to further involvement with writers from The Word Guild.

http://margueritec.wordpress.com